KEYS TO INVESTING IN COMMON STOCKS

Third Edition

Barbara Apostolou, Ph.D., C.P.A.
Arthur Andersen Distinguished Professor
Louisiana State University

Nicholas G. Apostolou, D.B.A., C.P.A.
U. J. LeGrange Endowed Professor
Louisiana State University

BARRON'S

All inquiries should be addressed to:
Barron's Educational Series, Inc.
250 Wireless Boulevard
Hauppauge, NY 11788
http://www.barronseduc.com

Library of Congress Catalog Card Number 99-42080

International Standard Book Number 0-7641-1301-1

Library of Congress Cataloging-in-Publication Data

Apostolou, Barbara.
    Keys to investing in common stocks / Barbara Apostolou, Nicholas G.
Apostolou. — 3rd ed.
        p.   cm. — (Barron's business keys)
    Includes index.
    ISBN 0-7641-1301-1
    1. Stocks—United States Handbooks, manuals, etc. I. Apostolou,
Nicholas G. II. Title. III. Series.
HG4921.A555 2000
332.63'223—dc21   99-42080
                                                     CIP

PRINTED IN THE UNITED STATES OF AMERICA

9 8 7 6 5 4 3 2 1

TABLE OF CONTENTS

1

WHAT IS COMMON STOCK?

As we enter the new millennium, we find ourselves in an economy with virtually ideal conditions—high growth, low unemployment, and startlingly low inflation. These factors have helped produce the longest bull market in history. The average yearly return on common stocks in the nineties, covering the period from 1990–98, was 17.9%. This performance on common stocks far exceeds that of the long-run average return of 11.2% for the period from 1926–1998. Our economy, bolstered by a dynamic technology sector, is the envy of the world. Incredibly, the U.S. government is now generating surpluses instead of deficits and has even cut capital gains taxes. In short, the nineties were a golden era for investors.

Over the long-term, stock prices are determined by two fundamental factors: (1) interest rates and (2) expected earnings. Other things equal, the lower the interest rates, the higher are stock prices and vice versa; the higher the expected earnings, the higher are stock prices and vice versa. The market is currently trading at a P/E ratio (price divided by earnings per share) in excess of 30, virtually an all-time high. The historical average for the market has been a P/E ratio of about 15 (see Key 15).

Many analysts have expressed concern about whether the U.S. market is in the midst of a speculative bubble comparable to the U.S. stock market in the late 1920s or the Japanese stock market in the 1980s. The Internet craze has reinforced this alarm, with stocks like Yahoo! up almost 80-fold in three years; Amazon up 45-fold in two; and eBay up 20-fold in just eight months.

How should the individual investor react? Very simply, every investor should focus on the long term. The U.S. economy will continue to grow, and corporations will continue to prosper. Common stock ownership gives investors a direct stake in the future of corporations. Ownership of common stock has proved over many years to be one of the best ways for investors to earn money. Even investors with limited capital are not shut out of this market.

Common stock represents shares of ownership in a corporation. Its owners bear the ultimate risk of loss and reap the benefits of success. However, dividends and assets upon dissolution are not guaranteed to common stockholders. Nonetheless, they are owners of the corporation and will be first to profit if the company is successful. The most popular way to invest in corporations is to own shares of common stock. More than 65 million people in the United States currently own stock in publicly traded companies.

Comparing investments. A successful investor should possess a sense of history, which tends to repeat itself, although not exactly in the same form. Markets are volatile, prices will fluctuate, but investors should be aware that opportunities are greatest when general pessimism prevails. On the other hand, a cautious stance generally should be assumed when the investment community is most optimistic. Looking at past trends in the markets assists in maintaining objectivity and a sense of perspective. An additional advantage is that alternative investments can be compared over time.

In the period from 1926–1998, common stocks increased at an average annual rate of 11.2%, substantially exceeding the return from long-term government bonds (5.3%) and U.S. Treasury bills (3.8%). Inflation over this 72-year period averaged 3% annually. If one dollar was invested in common stocks in 1926 (measured by using Standard & Poor's [S&P] Composite Index and assuming all dividends were reinvested), the investment would have accumulated to $2350.89 at the end of 1998. Meanwhile, one dollar invested in long-term government bonds would have grown to $44.18, whereas a dollar invested in Treasury bills would have increased to $14.94.

The evidence clearly demonstrates that in the long run, investments in common stocks have outperformed investments in the other capital markets. Although investors in common stocks assume greater risk than those who invest in government bonds, clearly their returns over the years have been much greater.

Finally, an issuance of a caveat is appropriate. The returns from common stock investments result from averaging the returns from many stocks. Poor choices of stocks can lead to losses even when the stock market is rising. Thus, the successful investor must be willing to expend the time and effort to select quality stocks and to diversify one's portfolio. Many publications, advisory services, and Web sites are available to assist the investor (see Key 24). In addition, investors can purchase mutual funds, which offer the twin advantages of professional management and diversification.

2

ASSET ALLOCATION

Most investors believe that the most important investing decision is the selection of individual stocks, bonds, mutual funds, and so forth. However, this decision is not nearly as important as generally assumed. The asset allocation decision—how dollars are split among stocks, bonds, and cash (including money market funds and short-term certificates of deposit)—is by far the most important determinant of investment performance. It turns out that what *portion* of total assets is invested in stocks generally is more significant than the individual stocks selected.

Although the importance of asset allocation over individual security selection may be surprising, this statement is not news to research academicians. A study by Brinson, Singer, and Beebower (published in the May-June 1991 issue of *Financial Analysts Journal*) assessed the performance of 82 large pension funds over a ten-year period. Their research shows that asset allocation determines more than 90% of the variation in total return. The individual stocks, bonds, and other assets that the pension funds picked did little on average to improve performance over the ten-year period.

Many investment advisers in recent years have recognized asset allocation as a positive approach to investment. Although it might be perceived as a gimmick to sell financial products, those advisers are onto something investors can ignore only at their own peril. Most investors tend to pay little or no attention to how they allocate their assets. All too often, they own a hodge-podge of mutual funds or common stocks bought at various times without consideration of how they complement each other. This approach is a big mistake. Proper attention to asset allocation can substantially reduce risk with little or no decrease in return.

The 30-year compound annual return (1969–1998), including price changes and reinvested dividends, for common stocks (as measured by the Standard & Poor's 500 Index) is 12.5%. But the average return masks some years of glittering returns and other years that were real downers.

Total returns soared more than 30% in seven of the years, but stocks were losing investments in six of the years, including the 26.47% plunge in 1974. Some investors may not be comfortable with this level of volatility or risk. Those investors who plan to cash in their stocks to finance the college education of their children or for their near-term retirement may find the possibility of a 26.47% plunge unacceptable.

That is where asset allocation comes in. Consider what would have happened if an investor had put one third of his or her money in stocks, one third in Treasury bonds, and one third in a cash equivalent investment such as Treasury bills. In the 30-year period, that investor would have lost money only four times, and the largest loss would have been less than 5%. Meanwhile, the compound annual return would have been about 10%, compared with 12.5% for an all-stock portfolio. Thus, history shows that sacrificing a 2.5% total return was accompanied by dramatically reduced risk.

If an investor is interested in making the most money possible and the time horizon is 30 to 40 years, then investing entirely in stocks makes sense. Although there exists about a 30% chance of loss in any one-year period (based upon results over the last 70 years), risk drops to 7% over any five-year holding period and only 3% in any ten-year period. In other words, extending the amount of time invested in the stock market greatly reduces risk. But most investors have shorter time horizons, and investing totally in stocks is too risky. For them, investing in several classes of assets such as stocks, bonds, real estate (personal residence at a minimum), and cash equivalents is a better approach.

Because asset mix is so important, some mutual fund companies now offer free services to help investors design their portfolios. These companies include Fidelity (*www.fidelity.com*), Vanguard (*www.vanguard.com*), Strong (*www.strong-funds.com*), and Berger (*www.bergerfunds.com*). They will either suggest an allocation upon completion of a questionnaire or provide a worksheet that assists in figuring out the appropriate mix.

The best combination of investments will vary depending upon age, income, health, employment stability, family size, and tolerance of risk. Each investor has to structure a strategy that fits his or her personal circumstances and this strategy will change over time and as financial position changes.

As a general rule, the further an investor is from his or her investment goal, the more money that should be in stocks. The closer to that goal, the more that can be allocated to bonds and money market instruments, such as Treasury bills. One simple, but effective, approach to common stock investments uses the following formula: 100 minus the investor's age. The amount represents the percentage of the portfolio that should be invested in stocks. For example, this formula means that a 40-year-old should have 60% of holdings in stocks.

When looking at how assets are allocated, all investments should be considered, including real estate, brokerage accounts, 401(K) money, individual retirement accounts, and certificates of deposit. After an investor has settled on the mix of investments desired, maintenance of the targeted percentage for the mix is all that is needed. To accomplish this goal, the allocation should be computed at least once per year. Downturns in the stock market can cause stocks to become a smaller percentage of the portfolio than desired. In that case, more cash should be put into stocks.

In making these asset allocation decisions, it helps to have an overview of how the three major categories (stocks, bonds, and cash equivalents) have performed historically. Stock and bond averages and indexes can provide this perspective. Current index information is readily available in local and national newspapers and magazines. The best periodical for historical information is the weekly publication, *Barron's* (800-228-6262).

The most complete information giving year-by-year total returns since 1926 for various stock and bond groups, as well as compound annual returns for different holding periods, is the yearly book *Stocks, Bonds, Bills, and Inflation* published by Ibbotson Associates (800-758-3557). The 1999 yearbook costs $100. This publication is available at many libraries.

\

3

STOCK EXCHANGES

Common stocks are traded primarily on nine stock exchanges in the United States. The largest stock exchange is the New York Stock Exchange (NYSE), which lists over 3000 companies with more than 260 billion shares issued and a market value of about $13 trillion. A smaller version of the NYSE is the American Stock Exchange (AMEX), which is located in Manhattan's financial district. The NYSE and AMEX are considered national exchanges. Common stocks also are traded on five major regional exchanges.

Generally, the stocks of the largest companies are traded on the NYSE, whereas those of the smaller companies are traded on the AMEX. The regional exchanges trade stocks of local corporations in addition to stocks listed on the NYSE and AMEX. The NYSE and AMEX generally are considered national in scope because of the large number of securities listed, the geographical dispersion of the companies listed, and the clientele they serve.

New York Stock Exchange. The NYSE dates back to 1817, when brokers adopted a constitution creating the New York Stock and Exchange Board, the predecessor of today's "Big Board." This constitution outlined membership requirements and commission rates and established procedures for trading and settling transactions. The brokers met in what was called a "call" market. Two times a day, the president of the board read the list of securities and members shouted bids and offers from their assigned chairs. Thus, the origin of the term "seat," which continues to signify membership on the NYSE.

The number of shares listed and the number of shares traded on the exchange have increased steadily through the years. Prior to the 1960s, the average daily trading volume was less than 3 million shares. Daily volume averaged about 15 million shares during the first half of the 1970s and exceeded 30 million by the end of that decade. Volume exploded during the 1980s, with daily volume usually exceeding 100 million shares. In the 1990s, volume continued to surge, with daily trading averaging over 800 million shares in 1999.

Stock exchange specialists are the center of the auction market for stocks. Their role is critical in maintaining an orderly market. A specialist is a member of the exchange who is assigned responsibility for about 15 different stocks. He or she must possess substantial capital and the knowledge to carry out this responsibility. Currently, there are about 430 specialists on the floor of the NYSE.

The requirements for listing on the NYSE are more stringent than the requirements on the other exchanges. A company must meet or exceed specified levels of net earnings, assets, and trading volume, and its shares must be widely held by investors. In addition, the NYSE requires evidence that trading interest in the company's shares is sufficient. Finally, a prospective listee also must agree to meet standards of disclosure, corporate governance, and stockholder participation.

American Stock Exchange. The AMEX was started by a group of individuals who traded unlisted shares at an outdoor location referred to as the Outdoor Curb Market. Typically, AMEX companies are smaller and younger than the companies listed on the NYSE. These companies frequently are considered emerging growth companies—companies that are not quite seasoned enough for the NYSE. Another characteristic of the AMEX is the number of smaller energy companies listed; the speculative nature of these stocks tends to make prices on the AMEX more volatile than those listed on the NYSE. In the last decade, the AMEX has introduced a variety of index products, which have become extremely popular (see Key 36).

Trading volume on the AMEX typically is about 5% to 7% of that on the NYSE. The disparity between the activity on the two exchanges is even greater when measured by the value of trading, because the price of individual shares on the NYSE tends to be higher than shares on the AMEX. In 1998, the AMEX merged with the NASDAQ to form the NASDAQ-AMEX Market Group.

Regional exchanges. Originally, these exchanges traded the securities of the regional companies located in their areas—thus, the origin of the name. However, the development of rapid communication expanded their scope. As a result, stocks on the NYSE and AMEX as well as local stocks are traded. For example, IBM and General Motors are both listed on the NYSE, but they are also listed on several regional exchanges. This dual listing permits local brokerage firms that are not members of the NYSE to trade shares of dual-listed stock using membership on a regional exchange. As a result, the local broker does not have to forgo part of the commission by trading through the NYSE. Most of the volume on regional exchanges currently results from trading in dual-listed issues.

The largest of the regional exchanges is the Chicago Stock Exchange. This exchange is a result of the merger of the Chicago, Cleveland, Minneapolis-St. Paul, St. Louis, and, in 1960, New Orleans Stock Exchanges. Its trading activity now exceeds that of the AMEX, making it the second largest organized stock exchange in the United States. Other prominent regional exchanges include the following:

- Pacific Exchange
- Philadelphia Stock Exchange
- Boston Stock Exchange
- Cincinnati Stock Exchange

4

OVER-THE-COUNTER MARKET

The term over-the-counter (OTC) originated when securities were traded over the counters in the storefront offices of various dealers from their inventory of securities. However, the term currently is an inaccurate description of how securities are traded in this market. The OTC market does not have centralized trading floors where orders are processed, like the NYSE and the AMEX. Instead, trading is conducted through a centralized computer-telephone network linking dealers across the country. Thus, these dealers can negotiate directly with one another and with customers.

The OTC market is based on a number of dealers buying and selling securities for their own accounts. The number of dealers that make a market in a particular security depends upon the popularity and the size of the issue. Each dealer making a market purchases securities from sellers at a *bid* price, while selling to buyers at a higher *ask* price. The difference between the bid and ask price is the *spread* that represents the dealer's profit.

When an investor trades OTC, an order is presented to a broker. If the broker acts as a dealer in that security, the broker will fill the order from inventory. Otherwise, the broker will act as an agent in contacting the dealer who offers the best price. The broker usually charges a commission for finding the dealer who makes a market in the security and assisting with the trade.

Securities traded. The OTC market is huge, including about 13,000 securities. Although OTC stocks represent many small and unseasoned companies, the range of

11

securities traded is great. The types of securities traded include common and preferred stocks, corporate bonds, U.S. government securities, municipal bonds, options and warrants, and foreign securities. There are several reasons why some securities are represented in the OTC market rather than being listed on one of the exchanges. Some securities issued by smaller companies cannot meet the more stringent requirements of the exchanges. Unseasoned issues of smaller companies typically are traded in the OTC market. Some of these eventually will qualify for listing on one of the exchanges.

In other cases, companies choose to have their securities traded in the OTC market even though they could fulfill the requirements for listing on the exchanges. Sometimes this choice is made because management prefers the negotiated OTC market, with its multiple dealers making a market in stocks, rather than the specialist system offered by the organized exchanges. Other companies may wish to avoid the financial disclosure and reporting requirements required by the exchanges. For instance, many large financial institutions continue to prefer to trade their securities in the OTC market.

NASDAQ. Prior to 1971, OTC quotations were compiled daily by the National Quotations Bureau (a private company), which published this data on what are commonly called "pink sheets." A major problem with this approach was the difficulty in getting current quotations from dealers. A broker had to contact various dealers to determine which one offered the best price for the investor. This approach was inefficient and time-consuming.

In 1971, the NASD started providing automated quotations through its National Association of Securities Dealers Automated Quotations (NASDAQ) system. This computerized communication network provides current bid and ask prices on about 6000 stocks. Through a computer terminal, a broker can instantly see the bid and ask quotations of all dealers making a market in a stock. The broker can then contact the dealer offering the best price and negotiate a trade directly.

Reading NASDAQ quotes. Two lists of NASDAQ securities are published in newspapers. The principal list is called NASDAQ National Market Issues, which includes more than half of the stocks in the NASDAQ system, with inclusion based upon a company's financial performance and investor interest in the stock. The list of National Market Issues (Exhibit 1) shows actual transaction prices, like those shown for exchange-traded issues. The information presented is in the same form as that presented for NYSE and AMEX issues (see Key 12).

In Exhibit 1, the first line displays the high and low price over the past 52 weeks. To the right, is the abbreviated company name, which is the exchange ticker symbol. The dividend yield percentage follows and it is computed by dividing the dividend paid by its closing market price. PE is the closing price divided by earnings per share for the last four quarters (see Key 15 for more on the price earnings ratio). Volume represents the number of shares traded and is quoted in hundreds (two zeros omitted). The next group of numbers displayed is the high, low, and closing market price of the stock plus its net change in price (the difference between the last closing price and the previous day's closing price).

EXHIBIT 1
NASDAQ National Market Issues

	52 weeks Hi	Lo	Stock	Sym	Div	Yld %	PE	Vol 100s	Hi	Lo	Close	Net Chg
	12 1/8	4 3/8	BrdgprtMach	BPTM		...	dd	38	9 1/8	8 7/8	9	-1/8
	12 3/8	7/8	BrigExplr	BEXP		...	dd	167	2 15/16	2 1/2	2 1/2	-1/8
	29 1/4	16 3/4	BrightHrz	BFAM		...	...	439	19	18 3/8	19	+5/8
	14 7/8	3 1/8	BrghtStrInfo	BTSR		...	...	1130	4 5/8	4 1/2	4 5/8	+1/8
	26 1/2	7	BrioTch	BVSI		...	dd	719	13 1/2	12 7/8	13	...
	14	7	BriteVoice	BTSR		...	12	554	13 1/16	12 15/16	13 1/16	+1/8
	8 3/4	2 1/2	BritBio	BBIOY		...	...	160	2 3/4	2 11/16	2 3/4	...
	25 7/16	14 3/4	BroadNtl	BNBC	.48b	2.0	16	116	24 9/32	24 3/16	24 1/4	...
sn	**177 1/4**	**16 3/8**	**brdcastcom**	**BCST**		**...**	**dd**	**4624**	**110 1/4**	**97 7/8**	**110**	**+10 3/4**
s	109 11/16	23 1/2	BroadcomA	BRCM		...	cc	15582	101 5/16	93 5/8	95 3/4	-2 5/8

Exhibit 2 presents the other NASDAQ list, which covers issues that do not meet all the listing requirements. Many of these smaller companies are eligible for the NASDAQ Small-Cap Issues list. Each listing includes the company name, dividend (if any), volume, closing price, and net change based on the previous close. (See Key 38 for a discussion of small-cap issues.)

EXHIBIT 2
NASDAQ SmallCap Issues

	Issue	Div	Vol 100s	Last	Chg
	FdltyHld n		41	21⅞	+⅜
	5AveChan		231	6⅞	-¼
	Finllnd		11	11¾	...
	Fd SVP		10	25/32	-1/32
	Fine.com		289	3 7/16	-⅛
♣	FinsMst		42	5½	-⅜
	Firearm		57	1	-1/16
	Firetct		372	1¾	-3/32
	FCmcBA	.36	6	26¾	+¼
	FCmcBB	.36	39	26⅞	+⅞
	FFdMN s		2	9¼	+¾
	FstLancas	.60	1	11 3/16	-3/16
	FtLesprt	.52	1	20¼	-¾
	FstPrior n		118	1⅝	...

NASDAQ is extremely successful. Its dollar trading volume makes it the second largest secondary securities market in the world, surpassed only by the dollar volume on the NYSE. NASDAQ has a share volume exceeding a billion shares per day, surpassing the volume of the NYSE, and it is the leading U.S. market for foreign listings.

NASDAQ listing requirements. NASDAQ has minimum requirements that must be met before securities are admitted to the system. These requirements are not as stringent as those of the NYSE or the AMEX. NASDAQ has different listing requirements for National Market Issues, Small-Cap Issues, and foreign common stocks.

5

THE SECURITIES AND EXCHANGE COMMISSION

Prior to the Great Depression of the 1930s, the federal government did little to regulate the securities markets. However, the collapse of the world financial markets fostered widespread criticism of their operation. In an effort to restore confidence, Congress intervened and established the Securities and Exchange Commission (SEC) in 1934 to administer federal laws to provide protection for investors.

The overriding purpose of these laws is to ensure the integrity of the securities markets by requiring full and fair disclosure of material facts related to securities offered to the public for sale. In addition, the SEC is empowered to initiate litigation in instances of fraud. The principal laws administered by the SEC are the Securities Act of 1933 and the Securities Exchange Act of 1934.

Securities Act of 1933. The Securities Act of 1933 provides for the regulation of the initial public distribution of a corporation's securities and for full and fair disclosure of relevant information concerning such issues to prospective purchasers. Various civil and criminal penalties are applicable to those who misrepresent information required to be disclosed under this act. Under its provisions, new issues sold publicly through the mails or in interstate commerce must be registered with the SEC. The SEC has special forms that must be used to disclose such information, including the following:

- Description of the registrant's properties and business
- Description of significant provisions of the security to be offered for sale and its relationship to the registrant's other capital securities
- Information about the management of the registrant
- Financial statements audited by independent public accountants

After the registration statement is filed, it becomes effective on the twentieth day after filing unless the SEC requires amendments. It is unlawful for the securities to be sold during this period. Registration statements are examined for compliance with applicable statutes and regulations. Moreover, if the SEC discovers that the registration statement is materially misleading, inaccurate, or incomplete, it can prohibit the securities from being sold to the public.

The SEC does not insure investors from losses. Nor does it prevent the sale of securities in risky, poorly managed, or unprofitable companies. Rather, registration with the SEC is designed to provide adequate and accurate disclosure of required material facts about the company and securities it proposes to sell so that investors can make informed decisions. A portion of the information contained in the registration statement is included in a prospectus that is prepared for public distribution. Every investor must be provided with a prospectus. The prospectus includes audited financial statements, information about the company's history, a list of its large stockholders, and other relevant facts. It is the investor's responsibility to obtain and read the information.

Securities Exchange Act of 1934. The 1934 act provides protection to investors by regulating the trading of securities of publicly held companies in the secondary market. Extensive reporting is required, along with continuous disclosure of company activities through annual, quarterly, and special reports.

Form 10-K is the annual report that must be filed with the SEC within 90 days after the end of the company's fiscal year. It contains a myriad of financial data, including the following:

- Basic financial statements and accompanying notes
- Management's discussion and analysis of financial condition
- Results of operations and an auditor's report

Form 10-Q is the quarterly report of operations that must be filed within 45 days of the close of each of the first three quarters. It contains condensed financial and nonfinancial information. Fourth-quarter operations are reflected in Form 10-K.

Form 8-K is a report of material events or corporate changes deemed of importance to the stockholders or to the SEC. Filing is required within 15 days of the occurrence of the event. An example of Form 8-K filing is when a company changes auditors.

A *proxy statement* includes information that must be provided to stockholders before they vote by proxy on company matters. It also provides information about the salaries and number of shares owned by the members of the board of directors.

Form 13-D must be filed with the SEC within ten business days if an investor acquires 5% or more of the outstanding common stock. The law is designed to protect against hostile takeover attempts and to keep the investing public aware of information that could affect the price of their stock.

These forms are available to stockholders or prospective investors upon request and on the SEC's Web site (*www.sec.gov*). Antifraud provisions call for harsh penalties for misrepresentations made in the various filings required by this act.

6

FEDERAL RESERVE BOARD

Money often is viewed as the force that moves the stock market, yet who controls that money? The Federal Reserve Board (Fed) fills this role in the U.S. economy. The Fed is the central bank, which oversees the activities of the nearly 3700 commercial banks that are members of the Federal Reserve System. These member banks accounted for 60% of all commercial bank deposits. With its broad supervisory authority over these banks, the Fed also controls the nation's money supply. Because changes in the money supply are so critical to the determination of interest rates and the state of the economy, the Fed is subject to intense media scrutiny.

Structure of the Fed. At the top of the Fed's organizational structure is the Board of Governors, located in Washington, D.C. The board consists of seven members appointed by the President of the United States and confirmed by the Senate. All appointments to the board are for 14-year terms. However, the President designates the chair and the vice-chair, who serve four-year terms with redesignation possible as long as their terms as board members have not expired. The chair occupies an especially powerful position, often cited as being second to that of the President.

Implementation of monetary policy. Monetary policy refers to the Fed's management of the money supply. The principal tools the Fed can use to regulate the money supply are described below:

1. *Open-Market Operations.* These operations control the money supply and are the most flexible

policy instrument, consisting of the purchase and sale of government securities on the open market. The transactions have a direct impact upon bank reserves and are employed continuously during each day as needed.

2. *Discount Window.* Discounting occurs when the Fed lends reserves to member banks. The rate of interest the Fed charges is called the discount rate; it is altered periodically as market conditions change or to complement open-market operations. It is primarily of interest as an indication of the Fed's view of the economy and of credit demand.

3. *Reserve Requirements.* Banks are required to maintain reserves against the money they loan. When reserve requirements are increased, the amount of deposits supported by the supply of reserves is reduced and banks have to reduce their loans. This tool is the least flexible and is seldom used.

Creation of money. The money supply is defined as currency in the hands of the public plus transactions accounts in depository institutions and traveler's checks. The Fed and depository institutions are the organizations that determine the money supply. Actually, currency (cash and coins) constitutes only a small percentage of the money supply. The money supply exists predominantly as accounts in banks. Most debts are primarily paid with checks or credit cards (that are followed by checks when payment is made). Cash typically is used for small transactions.

How is money created? Very simply, banks making loans create it. Assume that a bank makes a loan of $100,000 to a company that promises to repay after one year. The bank credits (or increases) the amount available in the company's checking account. Money supply increases by $100,000 as a result of this transaction. Subsequent repayment is made by deducting $100,000 from the company's checking account. This action reduces the money supply. The principle is simple: making loans increases the money supply, repaying loans reduces it.

What restricts a bank's capacity to make loans and create more money? Obviously, when individuals and companies have balances in their checking accounts, they write checks and withdraw cash from their accounts. Banks must maintain reserves either in the form of vault cash or deposits (checking accounts) with the Fed. The Fed requires that banks maintain reserves equal to a specified percentage of their deposits. Deposits are backed by reserves, whereas loans are not. The deposits represent a liability of the bank because the depositors can withdraw their money. The expansion or contraction of deposits increases or decreases the money supply.

Money supply and the stock market. The money supply tends to influence the level of stock prices through its effect on interest rates and economic activity. Other things equal, an increase in the rate of growth of the money supply tends to reduce interest rates, making stocks a more attractive investment. Alternatively, a curtailment in the growth rate of the money supply tends to hike interest rates, thus making investment alternatives (such as bonds) more appealing than stocks.

The Fed and inflation. When the Fed believes that inflation is a clear and present danger, it moves to hold down the growth of the money supply and raise interest rates (see Key 7 for an overview of inflation). Actions by the Fed that affect interest rates can significantly impact stock prices.

The clout of the Fed was demonstrated anew in the summer of 1999 after economic reports deepened investors' concerns that the strength of the U.S. economy would cause the Fed to raise interest rates. On June 11, the Dow Jones Industrial Average fell 130.76 points, or 1.23%, extending its loss for the four-day period from June 8 to 11 to 456 points.

Higher interest rates increase the cost of borrowing money, hurting investment and corporate profits. Also, higher interest rates increase the attractiveness of fixed-income investments. Thus, a hike in interest rates can have a chilling effect on both the economy and stock prices.

7

INFLATION

People often complain about the declining purchasing power of the dollar. Between 1970 and 1999, the general level of prices (as measured by the Consumer Price Index) has more than quadrupled. Inflation is an economic fact of American life, and no reputable forecaster assumes that this condition will change in the future. Inflation causes great concern because it results in the redistribution of wealth when it is not anticipated. For example, inflation tends to benefit borrowers at the expense of lenders whenever inflation rates are underestimated over the life of a loan. If $10,000 is borrowed for one year and the inflation rate for that year is 3%, the dollars of principal repaid at the end of the year have depreciated 3%. The borrower benefits by repaying less "real" dollars, whereas the lender receives dollars with diminished purchasing power. Hence, inflation causes the lender to lose.

Inflation also can have a corrosive effect on savings. As prices rise, the value of savings will decline if the rate of inflation exceeds the rate of interest. People on fixed incomes are particularly prone to the deleterious effects of inflation. The pensioner who retired in 1980 on a fixed pension found that the purchasing power of that pension had declined by about 50% as of 1999.

Finally, inflation affects investment returns. As a general proposition, common stock prices increase faster in periods of low inflation than in periods of accelerating inflation.

Measuring inflation. If inflation is defined as a rise in the general level of prices, how is it measured? This problem is solved easily when referring to the price change of one item, but it becomes trickier when dealing with a large number of prices, some of which have risen faster than others. Realistically, price changes for all the goods and services in an economy cannot be computed. Instead, a representative market basket of goods is selected, and the price changes of the market basket over time are computed. This calculation is obtained by using a price index that compares the current cost of the market basket of goods to the cost of those goods in the base year. Hence, the price index is derived as follows:

$$\text{Price Index} = \frac{\text{Current Cost of Market Basket} \times 100}{\text{Cost of Market Basket in Base Year}}$$

One way to gain an appreciation for the effect of inflation is to employ the "rule of 72." This method provides an approximate measure of the number of years required for the price level to double. The number 72 is divided by the annual rate of inflation:

$$\text{Number of Years for Prices to Double} = \frac{72}{\text{Annual Rate of Inflation}}$$

For example, the price level will double in approximately 24 years if the inflation rate is 3% per year. Similarly, inflation of 5% per year means that the price level will double in about 14 years. Savers can use this formula to estimate how long it will take their savings to double.

The Consumer Price Index (CPI). The CPI is the most widely cited index in the media. It attempts to measure changes in the prices of goods and services purchased by urban consumers. The Bureau of Labor Statistics computes the index monthly, based upon data collected in 85 cities from nearly 25,000 retail stores. The CPI reflects price changes of approximately 400 goods and services within eight broad categories: food, clothing, housing, transportation, medical care, recreation, education and communication, and other. The CPI is considered to be the most reliable measure of changes in the cost of living for American families. For the CPI, prices for 1982–84 represent the base year, which is set at 100. For example, the CPI measured 166.2 in April 1999, meaning the general level of prices, as measured by the CPI, had increased by 66.2% in the period from 1982–84 to April 1999.

Inflation and investment returns. Inflation impacts various investments differently. An asset that rises in price as fast or faster than the general level of prices is a good inflation *hedge*, or protection against loss due to the effects of inflation. Common stocks historically have been a better inflation hedge than bonds or Treasury bills. As a general proposition, research indicates that lower inflation leads to higher returns on stocks and bonds. In the years since 1960, when inflation has been 4% or less, total real returns on stocks have averaged more than 14% annually. However, when inflation ranges from 4% to 7%, the average real rate of return on stocks has dropped to less than 3%. Why is the market adversely affected by high inflation? Investors anticipate that the Fed will tighten its monetary policy, resulting in higher interest rates, a softer economy in the future, and lower corporate profits. Therefore, stock investors should be cautious when inflation threatens to accelerate.

8

BLUE CHIPS
AND OTHER TYPES
OF STOCK

Investors frequently describe stocks by categorizing them according to risk and return characteristics. Although these classifications are useful, investors should remember that there are no guarantees in the stock markets. Even the safest of all stocks, so-called "blue-chip" stocks, can be risky. Bethlehem Steel, a blue chip, continues to sell below the high of $60 it reached in the 1950s. No stock is consistently an excellent holding, and every investment involves risk. Investors should remember that a stock commonly classified as a growth stock may rapidly change to a speculative stock and vice versa. With this caveat in mind, stocks are frequently classified in the following five categories: blue-chip stocks, growth stocks, cyclical stocks, defensive stocks, and speculative stocks.

Blue-chip stocks. Blue-chip stocks are shares of common stock in a nationally known company that has a long history of profit growth and dividend payments. Some examples of blue-chip stocks include IBM, General Electric, Sears, and du Pont. Blue-chip stocks tend to be relatively high priced and pay a low dividend relative to their price because investors are willing to pay more for the lower risk associated with owning these stocks. These companies frequently are involved in multiple industries or in different segments of the same industry.

Many investors associate blue-chip stocks with the

stocks used to compute the Dow Jones Industrial Average, the well-known market index of 30 industrial companies listed on the New York Stock Exchange. The names of the stocks that comprise this index are listed in each Monday's issue of *The Wall Street Journal.*

Growth stocks. Growth stocks represent ownership in companies that have had, and are expected to continue to have, consistently superior earnings growth. These companies typically provide little dividend income because earnings are largely reinvested to finance future growth. The *Value Line Investment Survey* provides listings of growth stocks (stocks they define as having provided superior growth over the last ten years). Growth stocks are more likely to be found in the over-the-counter market (Key 4) because it is easier for companies to grow rapidly from a smaller base.

Although it is tempting to look for another Microsoft or Intel, investors should be aware of the greater risk in investing in growth stocks. By definition, growth stocks are *expected* to experience above-average growth. If these expectations are realized, investors can earn superior returns. But if the expected growth does not materialize, or if the rate of growth slackens, the stock prices can fall dramatically. Examples of prominent growth stocks include Microsoft, Cisco, and Home Depot.

Cyclical stocks. Cyclical stocks are stocks in an industry that is very responsive to the business cycle. Their earnings and stock prices can decline dramatically as the economy weakens and correspondingly strengthen as the economy picks up steam. Because their earnings tend to fluctuate more, cyclical stocks usually are riskier and more volatile than blue chips or defensive stocks. Stocks of noncyclical companies such as banks, food, and drugs are not as influenced by changes in the business cycle. Among the cyclical industries are auto, steel, copper, aluminum, machinery, and housing.

Defensive stocks. Defensive stocks are stocks in companies that are relatively immune to the ups and downs of the economy. These stocks have continually stable earnings in comparison to other stocks and their prices tend to fluctuate less than prices of other stocks. Thus, these stocks are less risky than cyclical stocks. The relatively stable market for their products accounts for the stability in their earnings. Examples of defensive stock groups include tobacco, food, and drugs. Investors should consider these stocks when anticipating market downturns.

Speculative stocks. Investments in speculative stocks offer a relatively large chance for a loss and a small chance for a large gain. Of course, a speculative stock is not automatically a bad investment. Usually there is a small probability of very substantial returns. A sophisticated investor may be willing to assume the greater risk in the hope of generating substantial returns. An investment in an oil exploration stock would be a good example. However, this type of stock should represent only a small proportion of an investor's portfolio—and the investor should have sufficient means so that any loss sustained would not mean financial hardship.

Stocks without a long-term record of profitability are questionable investments at any time. The penny-stock market is an example of a market to be approached with the utmost caution. A penny stock is one that trades for less than $1 per share. The North American Securities Administrators Association reports that penny-stock swindles cost investors at least $2 billion a year and are a major threat to small investors in the United States.

9

STOCK MARKET AVERAGES AND INDEXES

Most market participants—investors, speculators, and bystanders—get their first idea of how the stock market is doing from the news reports of the Dow Jones Averages and the S&P 500 figures. Even though these values are widely broadcast, very few people know what they actually mean—beyond the simple fact that up is good and down is bad.

Dow Jones Averages. The Dow Jones Industrial Average (DJIA) is the most widely followed stock market average. When the market trend is described, this index is almost always the one referenced. The DJIA was first calculated in 1884 by Charles Dow, who added the prices of 11 important stocks and then divided the total by 11. The average was broadened in 1928 to include 30 stocks, and since then companies have been added or dropped. Currently, the 30 companies represented in the DJIA are large, blue-chip companies. The divisor has been changed frequently to compensate for stock splits, stock dividends, and other factors, and is no longer equal to the number of stocks in the index.

Although the DJIA continues to be the most publicized index, Dow Jones also has indexes for 20 transportation-company stocks, and 15 utility-company stocks, in addition to a composite index of the 65 stocks in the three indexes. The names of the stocks included in the indexes are printed each Monday in *The Wall Street Journal*.

The Dow Jones stock averages are price weighted,

meaning that the component stock prices are added and the result is divided by another figure, the divisor. As a result, a high-priced stock has a greater effect on the index than a low-priced stock. A significant fluctuation in the price of one or several of the stocks in the index can distort the average. Thus, a 10% change on a $100 stock has a significantly greater impact on the index than a 10% change in a $20 stock. However, over the long term, the DJIA has been a useful indicator of the direction of the overall market.

Standard & Poor's Indexes. The six indexes compiled by Standard & Poor's Corporation are market weighted:

1. S&P 500 Stock Index (also called the Composite Index)
2. S&P 400 Stock Index (also called the Industrials Index)
3. S&P 1500 Index
4. S&P Utility Stock Index
5. S&P 600 SmallCap Index
6. S&P 400 MidCap Index

In a market-weighted average, both the price and number of shares outstanding enter into the computation. Use of this method means that stocks with a big market capitalization influence the indexes most. All of these indexes are assigned values of 10 for the base period of 1941–43.

S&P 500 is the most widely followed barometer of stock market movements after the DJIA. Originally it was computed with 233 stocks, but in 1957 it assumed a size of 500 stocks. On a daily basis, its movement is more representative of the movement of the stock market as a whole because of its larger size and the fact that the index is market weighted. It is composed of 400 industrial, 20 transportation, 40 utility, and 40 financial stocks. The index consists primarily of NYSE-listed companies, but it includes some AMEX and NASDAQ stocks.

NYSE Composite Index. The NYSE introduced the NYSE Composite Index in 1966 as a service to investors concerned with general price movements. The index is broad based because it reflects the overall price changes of all common stocks listed on the NYSE and measures changes in the aggregate market value of NYSE common stocks. The market value of each stock is obtained by multiplying its price per share by the number of listed shares. The sum of the individual market shares, the aggregate market value, is then expressed relative to a base market of $50—a figure approximating the average price of all common stocks on the base date of December 31, 1965. If the index stands at 600 as of a particular date, that means the average value of all common stocks listed on the NYSE on that date is 12 times as much as it was on December 31, 1965.

The NYSE also computes group indexes for industrials, utilities, transportation, and financial stocks. These indexes are computed in the same manner as the NYSE Composite Index, although a smaller number of issues is included.

American Stock Exchange (AMEX) Market Value Index. The AMEX Index is computed similarly to the NYSE Composite Index. It measures the performance of 800 issues on the AMEX. The base value of 50 is based on the close of trading on August 31, 1973, when this index was first introduced.

NASDAQ Indexes. The NASDAQ Indexes (supplied by NASDAQ) have become widely followed recently because of increasing interest in high-technology stocks. The NASDAQ Composite Index is market weighted and covers about 6000. NASDAQ also publishes several specialized group indexes covering specific industries.

Wilshire 5000 Equity Index. The Wilshire 5000 Index was first introduced in 1974 to meet the need for an index that reflects the performance of the organized exchanges and the OTC market. This index of 7200 stocks is the broadest index and the most representative of movements in the overall market. It is calculated in the same manner as the S&P 500 and the NYSE Composite Indexes. Its base value was at 1404.595 on December 31, 1980. On June 4, 1999, it stood at 12,152.34, indicating that the stocks in the index had increased almost nine-fold in value in 19 years.

10

MUTUAL FUNDS

For those investors who lack the time or expertise to manage an investment portfolio, an excellent investment alternative is to purchase shares in common stock (equity) mutual funds. A mutual fund is a pool of commingled funds contributed by many investors and managed by a professional fund manager in exchange for a fee. More than 6000 equity mutual funds are available to meet a wide range of investment objectives. There are funds that specialize in growth stocks, small-cap stocks, stocks of companies located in specific regions such as Asia, industries such as oil or health care, socially responsible companies, and dozens of other specific areas.

Advantages. Mutual funds offer several advantages that make them attractive for investors:

1. *Diversification.* A diversified portfolio is very difficult to achieve when funds are limited. A mutual fund offers the investor the opportunity to participate in an investment pool that can contain hundreds of different securities.
2. *Professional management.* Many investors lack the time or expertise to supervise their investments. Professionals who have the training and experience to make judgments about stock selection and timing manage mutual funds.
3. *Liquidity.* Funds can be easily traded. Quotes on the current value of funds are readily available in the financial section of most newspapers.
4. *Constant supervision.* Mutual fund managers handle all the details of managing the portfolio. These details include stock transactions, dividends, cash

exchanges, rights, and proxy statements. They arrange for dividend payments and update the performance and tax records for each investor.

Types of funds. Two basic types of mutual funds exist: closed-end and open-end. A *closed-end fund* issues a fixed number of shares. After the shares are issued, the company's shares trade on a stock exchange or in the over-the-counter market. Supply and demand determine share prices, which can be more or less than a share's intrinsic worth (net asset value). For some reason, most of these stock funds trade for less than their net asset value. Thus, investors who buy shares at a new fund's initial offering price generally have seen the prices of those shares drop, except in rapidly rising markets.

Open-end funds, by far the most popular type of mutual fund, issue or redeem shares at the net asset value (total assets minus total liabilities divided by the number of shares) of the portfolio. Unlike closed-end funds, the number of shares is not fixed, but increases as investors purchase more shares. These shares are not traded on any market and always are bought and sold at the net asset value of the portfolio. Typically, large mutual fund organizations manage families of funds that may include, for example, one or more growth funds, balanced funds, gold funds, money market funds, income funds, U.S. government securities funds, and small-cap stock funds. Usually an investor may switch from one fund to another within the same family of funds at little or no cost.

Mutual funds also can be divided into load and no-load funds. This distinction is based upon whether they charge investors a fee for buying shares. An investor in a load fund will pay a sales fee or commission, known as a "load," of up to 8.5% of net asset value, deducted from the amount of the investment. Thus, a $10,000 purchase of a 5% load fund means that $500 is deducted as a fee and only $9500 is actually invested.

No-load funds typically are purchased directly from

the investment company without brokerage firm involvement. No initial sales charge is deducted from the investment, so $10,000 invested in a no-load fund means that the entire $10,000 is actually invested. The performance of load funds has been compared with the performance of no-load funds, and there is no evidence that load funds perform better than no-load funds. An investor interested in short-term profits should unquestionably avoid high-load funds. Long-term investors should compare the track records of various funds, factoring into the calculation any commissions or other expenses.

Whether a fund is load or no-load is not to be confused with the annual operating expenses incurred by funds that are paid by all mutual fund investors. Information about a fund's annual expenses appears near the front of every mutual fund prospectus, the official sales document that must be sent to new investors.

Predicting which funds will perform well is exceedingly difficult. However, operating expense data is readily available. The purchase of a fund with low annual expenses will not necessarily get good performance; however, there exists an initial advantage over other investors who buy a similar fund with higher annual expenses.

A fund's expenses are stated as a percentage of a fund's average assets in any one year. On average, diversified stock funds charge 1.45% annually, but the range is from about 0.2% to 3.0% annually. An expense ratio of greater than 2.0% for a domestic stock fund is excessive.

Objectives of different funds. With more than 7000 open-end mutual funds available, investors have a wide variety from which to choose. However, it is extremely important that the objectives of the investor mesh with those of the fund. The Investment Company Act of 1940 requires that mutual funds state their objectives and make this statement available to interested parties. The objective of the fund can be changed only with the agreement of a majority of the stockholders. The following list summarizes the broad objectives of the different types of common stock funds:

1. *Aggressive growth* or *maximum capital appreciation funds* assume the greatest risk in the pursuit of profits. Some of these funds have outstanding long-term records, but investors must be prepared for sharp declines in net asset value during stock market drops. These funds are more willing to use speculative investment techniques, and may deliberately be less diversified than other funds to maximize the opportunity for capital gains. Only the more risk-oriented investors should participate in these types of funds.

2. *Growth funds* tend to be slightly less risky than "aggressive growth" funds, and their price should, therefore, be somewhat less volatile. These funds usually invest in companies that have exhibited long-term growth rates in earnings. These funds, like "aggressive growth" funds, are not concerned with dividends because they are likely to be small.

3. *Growth and income funds* are likely to invest in larger, stable companies that pay dividends and produce above-average earnings. Funds in this category tend to be less volatile and risky than funds in the first two categories. An investor can instruct the fund manager to automatically reinvest dividends into additional shares.

4. *Balanced funds* include both stocks and bonds to reduce risk. Funds with this objective are aimed at investors who are more risk averse. The inclusion of bonds in the portfolio should reduce the volatility of these funds and increase current income.

5. *International funds* invest primarily in foreign stocks or a mixture of foreign and U.S. stocks. The value of international funds is affected not only by changes in the prices of the foreign securities held, but also by the value of the dollar against foreign

currencies. An investment in foreign stock can lead to a profit or loss in two ways:

- The price of the stock in its local currency can advance or decline.
- Relative to the U.S. dollar, the value of the foreign currency may rise or fall.

The optimal situation is to have the price of the stock rise in the local currency and the value of the foreign currency rise against the U.S. dollar. (See Key 40 for more about foreign securities.)

Sources of information. Because mutual funds continue to proliferate, many investors are confused when making a decision about which one to purchase. Fortunately, there are several publications that regularly publish performance statistics. Both *Business Week* and *Money* publish frequent articles on mutual funds and useful quarterly statistics on performance. *Business Week's* annual *Mutual Fund Scoreboard Issue* is one of the best-selling single issues of the magazine and is highly recommended. In late August of each year, *Forbes* publishes a mutual fund survey of the performance records of all funds, including an "honor roll" of outstanding funds based upon such criteria as how they have performed in "up" and "down" markets. *Barron's* also publishes quarterly performance statistics in February, May, August, and November. Incidentally, all of these periodicals have excellent Web sites.

Over the last decade, both *The New York Times* and *The Wall Street Journal* have dramatically improved their coverage of mutual funds. These newspapers, along with *Investor's Business Daily*, do an excellent job of providing current data on mutual funds. They also present performance statistics that enable the investor to compare the different funds. The best known source of mutual fund information is *Morningstar*, which provides free mutual fund and other financial data and research on its Web site (*www.morningstar.net*). Its premium service is available at $9.95 per month. Those investors wanting an in-depth discussion of mutual funds should read John Bogle's *Common Sense on Mutual Funds* (John Wiley & Sons, 1999).

Recent growth. Millions of Americans, fearful of investing directly in common stocks, are investing in common stocks indirectly through the purchase of mutual funds. The mutual fund industry has multiplied in size, controlling more money than life insurance companies or savings and loan institutions. In 1999, total investment approached $6 trillion, up nearly 300% in just five years. In response, the number of funds grew to more than 7000, a startling increase from the 3100 just five years previously and less than 600 in 1980. At the end of 1999, about 45% of American households owned a mutual fund, up from only 6% in 1980.

11

BUYING STOCKS

An investor must act through a registered broker or dealer to buy or sell common stocks. Although these firms are closely regulated by the SEC, care should be exercised when selecting a brokerage firm and an individual broker or account executive, also known as a registered representative. Good brokers should be both knowledgeable about the market and effective in meeting the needs of their clients. Their duties include careful handling of purchase and sale orders, offering appropriate advice and research material about stocks, monitoring accounts to ensure there are no clerical errors, and taking care to see that money owed to customers is promptly mailed.

No special guidelines are available in selecting a good broker. Friends, relatives, and business associates may offer recommendations. A banker, lawyer, or accountant also might be a source of good information.

Types of brokers. Traditional, full-service brokers can provide information about the securities of companies that investors are considering. These brokers are members of firms with large research departments that make recommendations and offer advice to their clients. Merrill Lynch, Smith Barney, and PaineWebber are examples of large brokerage organizations.

Discount brokers provide fewer extra services to investors, but charge lower commissions than full-service brokers. Discount firms usually service investors who do their own research, know precisely what they want, and can make their own buy-and-sell decisions. Investors can save between 30% and 70% on their commissions by using a discount broker. Discount brokers simply execute orders, employing salaried order clerks who do not receive commissions. They also provide routine services. Examples of discount brokers include Charles Schwab and Quick & Reilly.

For even lower commissions, investors can choose "deep-discount" brokers. These brokers provide no-frills service, but execution of trading orders generally is fast and accurate. They make sense for investors who do their own research.

The fastest growing segment of the brokerage industry is firms engaged in on-line trading. On-line trading has had a revolutionary change on the way stocks are sold. Trades often are executed at a cost of 5% of what a traditional broker would charge (as low as $8 for a trade of 1000 shares). The ease and cost of execution accounts for why 30% of trades are currently being handled on-line (see Key 35).

The explosion of interest in on-line investing finally forced the hand of the largest full-service firm, Merrill Lynch. On June 1, 1999, Merrill Lynch announced that it will let its customers trade via the Internet for as little as $29.95 per trade, the same as its rival, Charles Schwab, starting December 1, 1999. Many of its customers want the advice of a broker, so Merrill Lynch is hoping that they will opt for a fee-based, full-service plan that charges a minimum of $1500 for unlimited trades and a broker's counsel. The fee will equal 1% of stock and mutual fund assets and 0.3% of cash and bond holdings.

Using full-service brokers. Investors pay a full-service broker approximately an extra $.30 to $.50 per share over the fee of a discount broker. Is the service worth it? To many, the answer has been *yes*. A full-service broker should be willing to provide the information necessary to make informed decisions. Investors should ask for research from the firm's analysts, data on P/E ratios, growth rates, insider buying or selling, and institutional ownership of companies. The broker also should provide *Standard & Poor's*

Stock Reports or *Value Line Investment Survey* in addition to its own research reports.

To minimize commissions, investors can make fewer transactions and concentrate on larger amounts of stock. Full-service firms typically charge fees of about 2% to 3% on trades above $3000, but on a $2000 trade the fee increases to 3% to 4% of the order, and at $500 it can be as high as 10%.

Opening an account. Opening an account with a brokerage firm is not significantly different from opening a bank account. A prospective investor will have to provide his or her name, address, occupation, social security number, citizenship, an acknowledgment that the customer is of legal age, and a suitable bank or financial reference. If the account is to trade in listed options, additional information is required. Most investors have cash accounts, which means that transactions are settled promptly without credit. Those customers who wish to gain leverage through the use of borrowed funds (see Key 32) use margin accounts. Only experienced investors should use this type of account.

Placing the order. When an investor decides to purchase stocks, the first step is to contact a broker and obtain a price quote. The quote often consists of two numbers: (1) the bid, or price that buyers are currently willing to pay, and (2) the ask, or price at which sellers are willing to sell. The investor has the choice of placing either a "market order," which means he or she will receive the best price available when the order is executed, or a "limit order," which means the trade can be executed only at a specific price. All orders are day orders—they expire at the close of business—unless otherwise indicated. An investor can choose to place a "good until canceled order," which means the order remains in effect on the broker's books until it is executed or canceled.

12

STOCK TABLES

Stock tables summarize trading activity in individual securities. For example, composite results of the previous day's trading in stocks listed on the New York Stock Exchange (NYSE) and on five regional exchanges are found in the New York Stock Exchange Composite Transactions Table (see Exhibit 3). This table typically is found in the financial dailies and, sometimes in abbreviated form, in local newspapers. It provides crucial information that should be evaluated before making a decision about buying any stock.

The name of the company issuing the stock is given in the third column. Because of space considerations, abbreviations for company names are used. The majority of the securities listed refer to common stock. Common stock represents the owners' equity interest in a corporation. Common stockholders share in the distribution of dividends according to the proportion of the total stock outstanding that they own. Typically, owners of common stock also have voting power and a residual interest in the assets of the corporation after claims of creditors have been satisfied.

The abbreviation of "pf" in the stock tables indicates preferred stock. Preferred stockholders receive a fixed dividend, which must be paid to them before any dividend can be paid to common stockholders. In addition, upon dissolution, the claims of preferred stockholders take precedence over the claims of common stockholders. Preferred stockholders usually do not have voting privileges.

EXHIBIT 3

New York Stock Exchange Composite Transactions Table

52 weeks Hi	52 weeks Lo	Stock	Sym	Div	Yld %	PE	Vol 100s	Hi	Lo	Close	Net Chg
49 1/2	18 3/4	♣ StrwdHtlRsrt	HOT	1.34e	3.7	dd	4560	36 1/8	35 3/16	36 1/16	+5/16
95 1/4	47 7/8	♣ StateSt	STT	.56	.7	29	4726	80 3/16	78 11/16	78 7/8	-1 1/16
23 1/2	13 1/2	StatnlsBcp	SIB	.40f	2.1	17	1674	18 3/4	18 1/8	18 3/4	+1/2
18 11/16	4	StationCno	STN	3.50	...	dd	719	17 1/4	16 3/4	17 1/16	+1/16
61 13/16	27 1/8	StationCno pf		.44	6.3	...	31	55 3/4	55 1/8	55 3/4	+1/2
31 5/8	12 3/4	Steelcase A	SCS		2.3	13	289	19 7/16	18 13/16	18 7/8	-3/8
32 3/8	16 15/16	Steinway	LVB	.60	...	12	12	23 15/16	23 3/4	23 15/16	+5/16
32 1/4	22 1/4	Stepan	SCL		2.5	11	329	24 1/2	24 1/8	24 1/8	-7/16
S	35 15/16	SterisCp	STE	.48	...	14	5524	17 1/2	17 1/8	17 1/4	...
28 3/8	16 3/4	SterlBcp	STL		2.3	13	84	20 5/8	20 1/4	20 1/2	+3/8
48 3/4	20 1/8	StringComrc	SE		...	dd	4268	39 1/4	37 7/8	38 1/4	-3/4
32 13/16	18 9/16	SterlSftwr	SSW		...	26	1772	23 3/8	22 13/16	23 1/8	+1/16
67 3/4	30 3/8	♣ StewInfo	STC	.32f	.8	6	127	40 1/4	39 3/16	39 3/4	-7/16
15 13/16	8 11/16	Stifel Fnl	SF	.12b	1.2	14	17	9 7/8	9 13/16	9 7/8	-1/16
42 1/8	19 3/8	♣ StoneWeb	SW	.60	2.1	dd	181	24 3/4	24 1/4	24 3/4	+1/2
23 1/16	14 1/8	StoneCont pfE			...	...	106	22 11/16	22 1/4	22 3/8	...
▲	37 11/16	19 5/8 StoneEngy	SGY		...	dd	369	38 3/4	37 3/8	37 7/8	+9/16

Abbreviations such as "s" are displayed in some of the entries. These abbreviations are explained in a section labeled "Explanatory Notes" located at the bottom of the newspaper page. For example, "s" denotes that a stock split or stock dividend of 10% or more has occurred in the past 52 weeks, whereas the letter "n" means that the security was newly issued in the past 52 weeks. The explanatory notes apply to both NYSE and AMEX issues and NASDAQ securities. The shamrock symbol (♣) indicates that an annual report and current quarterly report, if available, can be obtained by calling 800-654-2582.

The first column in the table reports the highest price paid for the stock over the last 52 weeks, excluding the previous day's trading. The second column gives the lowest price paid over the last 52 weeks. The four columns on the right give the high, low, and closing price for the day and the net change from the previous day. An upward arrow (▲) at the extreme left denotes that the price is the highest traded over the last 52 weeks, whereas a downward arrow (▼) at the extreme left indicates a new low for the previous 52 weeks. Any high or low price will be reflected in the 52-week high or low column (two columns on the left) the next day.

Other valuable information besides price is reflected in the table. Column 5, labeled "Div," is the annual cash dividend based upon the rate of the last quarterly payout. Extra cash or stock dividends are indicated by appropriate footnotes. The next column provides the yield percentages, determined by dividing the cash dividend by the closing price of the stock.

The P/E (price-earnings) ratio is computed by dividing the latest closing price by the latest available earnings per share (EPS), based upon diluted EPS (see Key 14) for the most recent four quarters. The P/E ratio is one of the most widely used measures for evaluating the price of the stock. It cannot be used alone when making decisions, however, for it should be compared with the company's past P/E ratios and with the P/E ratios of similar companies. The P/E ratio generally is an indication of how fast the market expects the company's earnings to grow. The higher the P/E ratio, the greater the potential growth in earnings should be (see Key 15).

Many investors use the P/E ratio of the Dow Jones Industrial Average (DJIA) as a standard of comparison. Thus, if the DJIA has a P/E ratio of 30 and an individual stock has a P/E ratio of 20, earnings are considered to be underpriced when compared to the market. Conversely, a P/E ratio of 40 indicates the stock is overpriced compared to the market. There always is a reason for these differences. These P/E ratios may be justified by the growth prospects and/or risk involved in purchasing the stock.

Investors generally prefer to buy stocks when the P/E ratio is as low as possible. Academic studies show that, on average, low P/E stocks earn better risk-adjusted rates of return than high P/E stocks. Because expectations are not as high for low P/E stocks, they are likely to be less affected by disappointing earnings than high P/E stocks.

Column 8 of Exhibit 3 gives the number of shares

traded in each stock, expressed in hundreds of shares. Thus, 75 means 7500 shares were traded that day. Transactions generally take place in units of 100 shares, commonly called a "round lot." A "z" before the volume figure means that the number represents the exact number of shares traded. Thus, "z75" means 75 shares were traded, not 7500. When the number of shares traded is less than 100, it is referred to as an "odd lot."

The Wall Street Journal has several additional features to its tables. Some of the quotations are boldfaced, which highlights those issues with price changes of 5% or more from their previous closing price. Underlined quotations indicate those stocks with large changes in volume compared with the issue's average trading volume. The underlined quotations are for the 40 largest volume percentage leaders on the NYSE and the NASDAQ system. For the AMEX, *The Wall Street Journal* highlights the 20 largest volume percentage gainers. Both of these features alert investors to stocks that may be of interest.

13

FUNDAMENTAL
ANALYSIS

Fundamental analysis involves an estimate of a security's value, called intrinsic value, by evaluating the basic financial and economic facts about the company that issues the security. After the intrinsic value is determined, it is compared to the current market price. If the current market price is less than the intrinsic value, a *buy* recommendation is issued. Alternatively, if the current market price is greater than the intrinsic value, the recommendation is to *sell* the security.

This form of analysis is in contrast to technical analysis, which looks at historical trends in stock price movements and other market variables to predict future stock prices (see Key 22). Technical analysts use indicators, charts, and computer programs to track prices and predict future trends. They often look upon the analysis of financial and economic variables as too burdensome and time-consuming to be useful in evaluating security prices.

Intrinsic value. The price at which a security should sell under normal market conditions is its intrinsic value. This price is determined by evaluating such factors as net assets (assets minus liabilities), earnings, dividends, prospects of future earnings and dividends (or risk), industry trends, and management capability. Critical to fundamental analysis is the evaluation of earnings, particularly expected future earnings. Most fundamental analysts cite the expectation of future earnings as the single most important variable affecting security prices.

The analysis of earnings is not a simple task. Fundamental analysts cannot use reported earnings alone as a guide to future earnings. Reported earnings are computed by accountants based upon certain prescribed rules known as generally accepted accounting principles, or GAAP. Earnings are affected by management discretion in making accounting estimates, such as determination of depreciation expense and cost of goods sold. Calculations ignore increments in the market value of assets—a property bought in 1970 for $1 million might be worth $20 million in 1999—and fail to take into account the omission of certain assets and liabilities from the financial statements.

Fundamental analysts must estimate "true" or "economic" earnings. This measure of earnings measures the change in wealth of an entity. Economic earnings frequently differ by more than 20% from the earnings reported by accountants. If developed properly, economic earnings should be a better measure of the capacity of the company to pay future dividends and generate future earnings.

The evaluation of earnings typically involves the appraisal of four earnings factors:

1. Level of economic earnings as well as reported earnings
2. Current and future dividends
3. Expectation of future earnings
4. Predictability of future earnings and dividends

Earnings that are predictable are more highly valued by fundamental analysts than earnings that cannot be accurately forecast. Similarly, earnings that follow a steady upward path are more highly valued than volatile earnings with the same overall upward trend.

Intrinsic value will change as factors that affect stock prices (e.g., earnings, dividends) change. Likewise, stock prices will change as the economic prospects of the company or its industry change. However, stock prices will fluctuate about the intrinsic value if it is accurately estimated. Factors external to the company, such as general pessimism or optimism, may cause temporary gaps between the intrinsic value and actual price of a security. Fundamental analysts believe that they can exploit these gaps.

Keep it simple. Peter Lynch, former portfolio manager of Fidelity Magellan Fund, largest of all mutual funds, wrote a book called *One Up on Wall Street*, which has become a classic. His thesis is that the individual investor actually has key advantages over professional investors. Institutional investors are at a disadvantage for two reasons:

1. They waste time justifying their decisions to their bosses. As a result, they tend to follow the herd.
2. A stock is not attractive until several large institutions recognize it. As a result, professional investors jump in after a stock has had a run-up in price.

Lynch states that the average person is exposed to interesting local companies and products years before the professional. Investors who keep their eyes open at work, at the shopping mall, and on the road can uncover interesting "stories" to exploit. Lynch offers sage advice to the average investor. As an example, he recommends investing only in companies with products and services that are easily understandable. He suggests that after a stock is purchased, it should be held for as long as the "story" that drew an investor to it in the first place is still valid.

14

EARNINGS PER SHARE

Earnings per share (EPS) probably is the most publicized and relied-upon financial statistic. Because of its importance, investors should know how EPS is computed as well as its usefulness and limitations. Many investors rely on EPS as a measure of performance without realizing its inherent dangers.

EPS has been called a summary indicator because it communicates substantial information about a company's performance or financial position in a single value. Many financial statement users focus upon summary indicators in response to the increasing difficulty in comprehending published financial statements. The accounting rules governing the presentation and content of financial statements often are arbitrary and complex, so that users are bewildered in attempting to grasp their significance. Many investors focus particularly upon EPS because they believe it provides critical information about stock prices and future dividends. However, overreliance on EPS can have several pitfalls. Misleading inferences can be drawn if the calculations that derive EPS on the income statement are ignored. Further, an analysis of the company's total operations and financial condition requires more information than can be garnered by examining only EPS.

Calculation of EPS. EPS is calculated by dividing total earnings by the number of common shares outstanding. (The term "earnings" is synonymous with "net income" and "net profit" to accountants who compute EPS.) EPS is reported at the end of the income statement; it is the proverbial *bottom line*.

The term, earnings per share, means the net income or earnings remaining for common stockholders after taxes and other deductions. For example, net income is reduced by the dividends due to the preferred stockholders:

$$\frac{\text{Net Income} - \text{Preferred Dividends} = \text{Net Income Available to Common Stockholders}}{\text{Average Number of Common Shares Outstanding}} = \text{Basic EPS}$$

However, this simple computation of EPS is inadequate when companies have convertible securities, stock options, warrants, or other financial instruments. These securities allow investors to convert their holding into common stock at some future time. The presence of these securities means that there is a potential increase in the number of common shares outstanding. In the computation of EPS, an increase in the number of shares outstanding results in a reduction (or dilution) of EPS. A doubling of shares, for instance, results in a 50% reduction. If companies possess a complex capital structure, a dual presentation of EPS is required. Accountants refer to these figures as "basic EPS" and "diluted EPS."

Conclusion. Investors view EPS as an important indicator of future stock price and dividends. As a result, it is widely reported in the financial press. Corporations are required to report EPS to their stockholders on a quarterly and annual basis. Reported earnings can have at least a short-term impact on the price of a stock, particularly when the figure differs from expectations.

Investors must be careful not to rely too heavily on EPS. Details in the income statement, such as trends in gross margin, may be more important than EPS. In addition, EPS may reveal little about the financial condition and cash flows of the company. It is one of the many pieces of information presented in financial statements that affect the value of securities and the measurement of management's performance. EPS is more valuable as a guide to evaluating a single company's performance over time.

Because EPS is affected by the choices of accounting methods, and one company's choices may be quite different from those of another company, comparisons of EPS between companies should be made with caution. In such a case, differences in EPS may be determined more by accounting conventions and rules than by economic substance.

Estimates of future earnings, usually supplied by Zacks (*www.zacks.com*) and First Call (*www.firstcall.com*), are now widely available on different Web sites. Two of our *free* favorite starting points for information about stocks are Yahoo!Finance (*www.quote.yahoo.com*) and Quicken (*www.quicken.com*).

15

PRICE-EARNINGS RATIOS

Is a stock a bargain? Is the market as a whole under-valued or overvalued? One of the most widely used tools to make this assessment is the price-earnings (P/E) ratio. A P/E ratio is simply a stock's price divided by the company's earnings per share over the most recent four quarters. A high P/E ratio indicates that the market expects exceptional earnings growth, and a low P/E ratio suggests that the market anticipates low earnings growth. The P/E ratio for each stock is listed in the daily stock tables of most major newspapers (see Key 12). Generally, the higher the P/E ratio, the more optimistic (bullish) investors are about a company's prospects, although abnormally high P/E ratios of 50 or more may indicate that the company has taken a one-time charge to earnings, skewing the ratio.

The P/E ratio of any stock that is fairly priced should correspond to the growth rate of earnings. If McDonald's has a P/E of 20 and Cisco of 60, that would indicate that the market expects Cisco's earnings growth to be about three times as great as McDonald's. A P/E ratio that is half the growth rate is generally regarded as very posi-tive, whereas a P/E ratio that is twice the growth rate often is an unattractive prospect. If an investor is con-sidering the purchase of a particular stock, it is useful to know how much is being paid for the earnings compared to what others have paid in the past. The information about earnings growth and P/E ratio histories can be obtained from the *Value Line Investment Survey*, which is available in most large libraries or from a broker. In addition, many libraries have books published by Standard & Poor's, Moody's, and other financial services that track the earnings records of NYSE, AMEX, and NASDAQ-listed companies.

Stocks with high P/E ratios, implying high expected future earnings growth, can be risky investments. These stocks experience sharp price drops if earnings do not materialize as expected. Stocks with low P/E ratios may be less risky because the market has a lower expectation of future earnings growth. Of course, in some of these stocks the earnings trend is downward, carrying the possibility that the price trend will follow that same direction.

P/E ratio of the market. The stock market as a whole has its own collective P/E ratio, which can be an indicator of whether that market is overvalued or undervalued. During the past 50 years, the P/E ratio of Standard & Poor's (S&P) 500 Stock Index has ranged between 7 and 35. Historically, the average P/E ratio of the market has been about 15. In 1999, the market was at an all-time high not only in absolute numbers but also in its P/E ratio of 35. Exceptional earnings growth and low interest rates account for much of this stellar performance. However, investors should be aware of how exceptional the recent period has been.

In the last 17 years (through 1998), stocks have been down in only one year (1990), and in only four did they underperform Treasury bills. Over the last century, stocks have been down in nearly 30% of the years and outperformed Treasury bills about 60% of the time.

Interest rates have a significant effect on the market P/E ratio, because investors find stocks more attractive when interest rates are low and bond prices are high. Conversely, higher interest rates make bonds more attractive, so that investors shift money from stocks to fixed-income securities. Aside from interest rates, a herd mentality periodically grips the market, driving P/E ratios abnormally high or low. Investors should periodically monitor the P/E ratio of the S&P 500 Index, which is reported on a weekly basis in *Barron's* and *The Wall Street Journal* and daily in *Investor's Business Daily.*

16

INCOME STATEMENT

The income statement reports revenues and expenses incurred over a specific time period. It provides very useful information as to the performance of a company for a given time span. (Investors should remember that, *in the long run*, there is a strong relationship between earnings growth and the performance of the stock.) After all expenses are subtracted from all revenues, the remainder is net income, or the *bottom line*. The terms income, earnings, and profits are used interchangeably by accountants. The profit (or loss) is shown at the bottom of the income statement, both as a lump-sum figure and as a per-share amount.

Why is the income statement so important? The primary reason is that it provides investors, creditors, and others with information to predict the amount, timing, and uncertainty of future earnings. Accurate prediction of future earnings permits the assessment of the economic value of the company, the probability of loan repayment, and the likelihood of dividend payout. The income statement also is helpful in estimating future cash flows of a company.

Financial ratios. Although there are many financial ratios used by analysts, some of the most prominent ones are based on amounts reported in the income statement. The most widely publicized of all financial ratios is earnings per share (see Key 14). Other important ratios using income statement values are:

- *Gross profit margin.* This ratio is computed by dividing gross profit by net sales for the period. The equation for this relationship is:

$$\text{Gross Profit Margin} = \frac{\text{Gross Profit}}{\text{Net Sales}}$$

This ratio measures the ability of a company to control inventory costs and to absorb price increases through sales to customers.

- *Return on equity.* The ultimate measure of operating success is the return on equity, which refers to common stockholders' equity. It is calculated by dividing net income by the equity of common stockholders. In equation form:

$$\text{Return on Equity} = \frac{\text{Net Income} - \text{Preferred Dividends}}{\text{Common Stockholders' Equity}}$$

To obtain common stockholders' equity, it is necessary to subtract from total stockholders' equity the stockholders' equity that pertains to preferred stock.

- *Price-Earnings ratio.* The price-earnings (P/E) ratio is widely used by analysts in discussing the investment possibilities of different stocks. It is computed by dividing the market price of the stock by the earnings per share (EPS):

$$\text{Price-Earnings Ratio} = \frac{\text{Market Price of Stock}}{\text{Earnings Per Share}}$$

High P/E stocks *usually* are characterized by greater growth potential than low P/E stocks.

- *Payout ratio.* The payout ratio is the ratio of cash dividends to net income.

$$\text{Payout Ratio} = \frac{\text{Dividends Per Share}}{\text{Earnings Per Share}}$$

Many investors select stocks with a fairly substantial payout ratio. However, others are more concerned with appreciation in the price of the stocks. High growth companies tend to be characterized by low payout ratios because they reinvest most of their earnings.

Investors should not use ratios in isolation. Rather, they should be considered relative to the ratios of other companies in the industry or to the relative performance of a single company over time.

17

CASH FLOWS

Another financial statement required by accounting standards is the statement of cash flows. This statement is presented along with the income statement and balance sheet. The adoption of this statement was spurred by the dissatisfaction of many investors with reported earnings as a measure of a company's performance. One of the problems with reported earnings is that the final figure is affected by the accounting methods used and may not be indicative of the underlying cash flows. The SEC requires that the statement of cash flows disclose results for the recent three years. Investors should examine the trend over the last three years.

Purpose of the statement. The primary purpose of the statement of cash flows is to report information about a company's cash receipts and cash payments during a period. It is useful because it provides information about (1) sources of cash during the period, (2) uses of cash during the period, and (3) change in cash balance during the period. Although the statement of cash flows provides information about the current period's cash receipts and cash payments, it cannot be used alone to provide insight into future cash flows. This limitation arises because current cash receipts result from cash payments made in past periods, whereas cash payments made currently frequently have the aim of increasing future cash receipts. As a result, the statement of cash flows must be considered in combination with the balance sheet and income statement to predict future cash flows.

Classifications. The statement of cash flows is classified into three major categories:

1. *Operating activities,* including the typical daily transactions involving the sale of merchandise and the providing of services to customers. Examples include the cash receipts from the sale of goods or services and cash payments to suppliers for purchases of inventory.
2. *Investing activities*, including lending money, collecting on those loans, or acquiring and disposing of productive long-lived assets.
3. *Financial activities*, including obtaining cash from creditors, repaying the amounts borrowed, or obtaining capital from owners and providing them with dividends.

Focal number. The cash flow from operating activities is the first and foremost source of a company's cash because they involve the sale of goods and/or services. If operating cash flow is not the primary source of a company's cash flow, the company could be in trouble. The bigger the contribution of operating cash flow to a company's cash needs, the better.

Free cash flow. There is increasing use in the financial press of the term "free cash flow." Although there is as yet no universal definition of this concept, the most widely used version is as follows:

Free cash flow =
Operating cash flow* – capital expenditures

as reported in statement of cash flows

Free cash flow is an extremely important computation for takeover specialists in evaluating different companies. This amount gives raiders the clearest picture of how much cash would be available to meet the debt incurred in an acquisition.

18

BALANCE SHEET

The balance sheet is a financial statement that reveals the financial condition of a company at a particular point in time, usually the end of a quarter or fiscal year. It is useful to investors because the relationship among different parts of the balance sheet provides evidence as to a company's financial strength, which in turn can furnish clues to its future performance. The balance sheet summarizes what a company owns (assets) balanced by what a company owes to outsiders (liabilities) and to owners of the enterprise (owners' equity or stockholders' equity). In equation form, the balance sheet is represented as follows:

$$\text{Assets} = \text{Liabilities} + \text{Stockholders' Equity}$$

By definition, the balance sheet must always balance, meaning assets must always equal liabilities plus stockholders' equity. This relationship is crucial to understanding the balance sheet. For example, if a company has assets of $3 million and liabilities of $1 million, then stockholders' equity will be $2 million. An alternative view of the balance sheet equation is to rearrange liabilities:

$$\text{Assets} - \text{Liabilities} = \text{Stockholders' Equity}$$

This form of the equation reflects the fact that stockholders have a claim to assets only after creditors' claims are satisfied.

Assets. The economic resources expected to provide future benefits to the company are called assets. A balance sheet is classified so that similar items are grouped together to arrive at significant subtotals. Assets are divided into three categories:

1. Current assets
2. Property, plant, and equipment
3. Intangible assets

Current assets include cash plus other assets expected to be converted into cash within one year. Current assets are the assets used up and replenished continuously in the ongoing operations of the company. The most prominent current assets are cash, marketable securities, receivables, and inventories.

Property, plant, and equipment includes assets with relatively long lives. Assets within this category, except land, are depreciated over their useful lives. Depreciation is a method of allocating the cost of an asset over its productive life. The total depreciation expense recorded is called *accumulated depreciation*. On the balance sheet, the balance for property, plant, and equipment is always shown after a deduction for (or net of) accumulated depreciation.

Intangible assets embody valuable rights to the company even though they have no physical substance. Typical examples are patents, trademarks, franchises, and copyrights. Patents, for example, provide the holder with the exclusive right to use, manufacture, and sell a product or process for a period of 17 years without interference or infringement by others.

Liabilities and stockholders' equity. Liabilities are economic obligations of a company to outsiders. There are two types:

1. Current liabilities
2. Long-term liabilities

Current liabilities are those liabilities usually payable within one year. *Long-term liabilities* will come due after one year.

Stockholders' equity is the owners' or stockholders'

interest in the company. Within this category is the retained earnings account, which represents the undistributed cumulative net income or losses, less any dividends distributed. The retained earnings balance provides no indication of the amount of cash a company possesses. It represents funds the company has reinvested in its operations, as opposed to making distributions to stockholders in the form of dividends.

Limitations of the balance sheet. The balance sheet provides information about the nature of resources owned, the obligations owed to outsiders, and the amounts to which stockholders are entitled. This information is of key importance to an analyst who is trying to make intelligent judgments about the risk associated with investments in the company and about the probability (and amount) of future cash flows to be generated. However, anyone examining a balance sheet should be aware of their limitations.

The balance sheet does not reflect the current market value of assets. Most assets are shown at their original cost. The exceptions are receivables, marketable securities, and long-term investments. For example, land acquired in 1940 will appear in the 1999 balance sheet at its original 1940 cost. If its market value is ten times its original cost, this information will not appear in the balance sheet.

In addition, *the balance sheet omits items that are of financial value to the business but cannot be recorded objectively.* For example, the value of a company's human resources or its brand names is not reflected on the balance sheet because of the difficulty in measuring the value of these assets.

19

FINANCIAL RATIOS

A financial ratio is computed by dividing one number in the financial statements by another. Many financial ratios can be computed based upon the values on the balance sheet. A few are widely reported in the financial press:

- *Book value per share.* This ratio is the amount each share would be worth if the company liquidated at the amounts reported in the balance sheet. It is computed with the following formula:

$$\text{Book Value Per Share} = \frac{\text{Common Stockholders' Equity}}{\text{Number of Common Shares Outstanding}}$$

Common stockholders' equity is computed by taking total stockholders' equity and reducing it by the amount of stockholders' equity attributable to preferred stock. This ratio becomes less relevant if the valuations on the balance sheet do not approximate the current market value of the assets.

- *Current ratio.* This ratio is the most commonly used measure of short-run liquidity. It is computed with the following formula:

$$\text{Current Ratio} = \frac{\text{Current Assets}}{\text{Current Liabilities}}$$

Although both the numerator and denominator are dollar amounts, it is usually expressed as coverage of "so many times." For example, if current assets are $200,000 and current liabilities are $100,000, the current ratio is 2, or "two times." This ratio offers an indication of the company's ability to pay debts as they become due.

- *Debt ratio.* This value is computed by dividing total liabilities by total assets:

$$\text{Debt Ratio} \quad = \quad \frac{\text{Total Liabilities}}{\text{Total Assets}}$$

The debt ratio indicates the extent of the company's financing with debt. The use of debt involves risk because it requires fixed interest payments and eventual repayment of principal. When debt is used successfully, however, it provides benefits to stockholders. When the earnings from the use of resources borrowed exceed the interest and principal repayment, management has employed financial leverage successfully.

To offer a simple example, a manufacturer might decide to purchase a high-speed machine that would quadruple a plant's production of widgets, from 100,000 to 400,000 per month. If the machine cost $500,000 and was financed by an 11% loan payable over a period of five years, the monthly cost to the manufacturer before taxes would be $10,871.20. Thus, the extra 300,000 widgets produced each month would have to bring in a profit of at least $11,000 per month for the machine to be a worthwhile acquisition.

20

DIVIDENDS

Dividends are distributions of earnings to stockholders. Although most commonly in the form of cash or stock, dividends also can consist of property such as merchandise, real estate, or investments. Typically, companies can only declare dividends out of earnings, although some state laws permit the declaration of dividends from sources other than earnings. Dividends based on sources other than earnings sometimes are described as "liquidating dividends" because they are a return of the stockholders' investment rather than earnings.

Cash dividends. Cash dividends are the portion of earnings distributed to stockholders in the form of cash. They become a liability of the company after the board of directors approves or declares their future payment. Cash dividends usually are paid on a quarterly basis shortly after the dividend resolution has been approved by the board. Dividends cannot be paid immediately because the ongoing purchases and sales of the company's stock require that a current list of stockholders be prepared. For example, a resolution approved at the April 10 (declaration date) meeting of the board of directors might be declared payable on May 5 (payment date) to all stockholders of record as of April 25 (record date). The period from April 10 to April 25 provides time for any stock transfers in process to be completed and registered with the transfer agent. Investors owning the stock as of April 25 receive the dividend even if the stock was sold between April 25 and the date of payment, May 5. Therefore, on the day after the record date, the stock trades "ex-dividend"—without the current dividend—and usually falls slightly in price to compensate for the difference.

Payout ratio. The payout ratio is the ratio of cash dividends to net income (see Key 16). It is the portion of net income or earnings that the company's board of directors pays out in cash. The payout ratio varies widely. Smaller, high-growth companies tend to have low payout ratios because they have a stronger need to reinvest the cash generated from operations in capital facilities to finance future growth. However, many mature, profitable, lower-growth companies follow the high payout formula.

Dividend yield. The dividend yield percentage often is reported in the stock tables of major newspapers (see Key 12). This value is obtained by dividing the annual cash dividend by the closing price of the stock. The annual cash dividend is based upon the rate of the last regular quarterly payout. If the dividend in the last quarter was $.25 per share, the annual dividend is assumed to be $1.00. This value can be compared with the dividend yield of other stocks and with the interest paid on bonds and other debt instruments.

Stock splits and stock dividends. A stock split is the issuance to stockholders of new shares of stock. For example, a two-for-one split gives each stockholder two new shares for each share held. A stock dividend is simply a small stock split. For example, if a corporation issues a 5% stock dividend, the owner of 100 shares will receive an additional five shares of stock. Essentially, all that happens with these transactions is that the total number of shares outstanding increases, the price per share decreases proportionately, and the total value of the investors' common stock remains unchanged.

If nothing is really to be gained through stock dividends or stock splits, what is a company's underlying motivation for such actions? For one thing, an unsupported tradition on Wall Street is that a stock price of between $25 and $50 is most appealing to investors. In addition, stockholders seem to react positively to

65

distributions of additional shares even if the total value of their holdings remains unchanged. The price of the stock seems "cheaper" after the split than before, especially in a company with a rising earnings trend. Stock splits often occur following run-ups in the price of the stock. Alternatively, companies often issue stock dividends when cash dividends are unaffordable.

Dividends matter. In discussions of investing for maximum return, increases in stock prices get all the attention. The focus is usually on finding a stock that will multiply in value rather than finding one that delivers a steady stream of dividends. Many of the hottest stocks in recent years pay little or no dividends.

Price appreciation has trounced dividends in determining total returns in recent years. Over the past decade, dividends and gains from the reinvestment of those dividends accounted for just 16% of the annual total return of the S&P 500 Stock Index. In the summer of 1999, the S&P 500 Stock Index was yielding 1.2%, an all-time low. Dividends have been much more significant over longer periods, however. From 1926 through the end of 1998, about 40% of the 11.2% annual return on common stocks was attributable to dividends.

The recent de-emphasis on dividends is supported by U.S. tax regulations. Increases in stock prices are not taxed until a stock is sold, and then they are subject to favorable capital-gains rates no higher than 20%, as long as the stock is held for more than 18 months. Dividends are taxed at ordinary income tax rates as high as 39.6%. Rather than avoid dividend-paying stocks because of taxes, though, they can be held in a tax-deferred account, such as an individual retirement account (IRA).

21

DIVIDEND REINVESTMENT PLANS (DRIPs)

Those investors who wish to buy shares of common stock as cheaply as possible have as an alternative: dividend reinvestment plans (DRIPs). More than 1100 companies offer DRIPs, and the number continues to increase every year. DRIPs are tailor-made for long-term buy-and-hold investors.

A DRIP involves the automatic reinvestment of stockholder dividends in more shares of the company's stock. The process eliminates the brokerage firm as an intermediary between the individual's desire to buy shares and the company's desire to sell shares. Instead of sending cash dividends to participating investors, the company applies those dividends to the purchase of additional shares of stock. Plan members can choose to have all or a portion of their dividends reinvested automatically. DRIP instructions can be changed at any time. Participants are able to buy additional stock without calling a broker and without any commissions. About 100 of the DRIP companies will even sell the additional shares at a discount, usually 3% to 5% from its current market price.

Plan mechanics. DRIPs primarily are intended to serve existing stockholders. These plans are initiated by companies for several reasons. Some companies wish to attract more individual long-term investors. Retailers see DRIPs as a way to increase customer loyalty by encouraging more of their customers to become stockholders.

Some companies administer their own DRIPs. Most companies, however, appoint an outside party to serve as the administrator for the plan. The minimum requirement for enlisting in the plan typically is to own only one share. The share must be registered in the investor's name; owning a share registered in the name of a brokerage house will not suffice. If the shares are in a broker's name, they should be transferred to the investor's name.

A company will normally send a DRIP prospectus or description and an authorization card after an individual becomes a registered stockholder. These items can be requested by calling the company and asking for stockholder relations or accessing the company's Web site. The plan prospectus should be read closely. The prospectus will provide information on enrollment procedures, initial investments, reinvestment of cash dividends, withdrawal from the plan, sale of shares, price of shares, and reports to participants.

Costs. The basic plan involves the reinvestment of all dividends of stock registered in the individual's name. Under some plans, a choice to reinvest only a portion of the dividends may be available. The remainder of the dividends can be directly deposited in a bank account by electronic transfer or sent by check.

Many plans permit the purchase of additional shares in addition to reinvesting dividends. For example, Exxon allows the purchase of its stock as frequently as once per week and in increments as small as $50. Because Exxon charges no commission, the full investment goes to the purchase of shares. The Exxon plan allows the amounts invested to vary. This option gives the purchaser flexibility to adjust investment activity to keep pace with changing investment needs. As do an increasing number of plans, Exxon permits the establishment of individual retirement accounts (IRAs) that invest in Exxon's stock.

Many companies do not charge for share purchases from both reinvested dividends and optional cash payments. Other companies might have service fees of about $5 per transaction. If brokerage commissions are charged for investors who also buy extra shares regularly for cash, they are levied at institutional rates, which are considerably lower than an investor would have to pay on his or her own.

Participants may request the sale of shares by giving written instructions to the administrator. Exxon imposes a $5 administrative charge and a brokerage commission (currently about $.10 a share).

Super DRIPs. The hottest topic in the world of DRIPs is the introduction of *super DRIPs* by many major companies including about half of the 30 companies that are included in the Dow Jones Industrial Average. Traditionally, DRIPs have only been open to current stockholders, which meant that stockholders had to buy their initial shares from a broker and pay a commission. Now, however, under super DRIPs or no-load programs, companies will sell investors those first shares commission-free.

For additional modest fees, super DRIPs are providing a wide range of services including the following: borrowing against the stock, creating IRAs with the shares, buying shares at a discount, reinvesting dividends, and prearranged daily or weekly sales of the holdings. Some plans will even automatically debit a bank account for purchases, much like mutual funds.

Taxes. The tax status of DRIPs is not one of their advantages. Participants are subject to taxes whether dividends are received in cash or are reinvested. If the investor buys at a discount, the value of the discount is also taxable. Further, any brokerage fees paid by the company are considered dividend income and are taxed. Plan members receive 1099-DIV forms each year from the company identifying the amount of income to be reported to the IRS.

Further information. A stock should not be purchased just because it participates in a DRIP. DRIPs are a stockholder bonus in a company with promising long-term growth prospects. They do not make sense for traders who like to anticipate market turns. New shares can be purchased only at certain times, and it may take at least ten days to sell the shares.

Charles Carlson (219-931-6480) publishes a directory of DRIP plans, costing $10.95. He also has a Web site at *www.dripinvestor.com*. The *AAII Journal* published by the American Association of Individual Investors (AAII) (800-428-2244) publishes an annual list of DRIP plans, usually in the June issue. The *AAII* is an independent not-for-profit organization of 170,000 investors that does an excellent job of education and research (see Key 47).

22

TECHNICAL ANALYSIS

Technical analysis is the attempt to predict future stock price movements by analyzing the past sequence of stock prices. Technical analysts dismiss such factors as the monetary and fiscal policy of the government, economic environment, industry trends, and political events as being irrelevant in attempting to predict future stock prices. Their concern is with the historical movement of prices and the forces of supply and demand that affect those prices.

Technicians place very little faith in accounting data, citing such weaknesses as the lack of comparability of financial reports because of alternative acceptable methods of accounting and the use of original cost to value assets on the balance sheet. Further, they say that the time it takes to process and evaluate accounting data is much too long. Technical analysis leads to much quicker decisions.

Techniques. Technical analysts use a wide variety of methods as they attempt to predict future prices. Many rely on charts and look for particular configurations that are supposed to have predictive value. Entire books have been devoted to interpreting charts. Some analysts focus upon the measurement of investor psychology, whereas others monitor the activities of mutual funds or sophisticated investors.

The tools and techniques of technical analysis are endlessly varied. However, technical analysts tend to agree on the following underlying principles:

1. Market value is entirely determined by the interaction of demand and supply.

2. Both rational and irrational factors govern demand and supply.
3. Stock prices generally tend to move in trends that persist for significant periods of time.
4. Changes in trends are caused by the shifts in demand and supply.
5. Chart patterns often tend to recur, and these recurring patterns can be used to forecast future prices.
6. Shifts in demand and supply can be detected in charts of market prices.

Compared to fundamental analysis. Technical analysis frequently is contrasted with fundamental analysis (see Key 13), which attempts to measure the intrinsic value of a security by analyzing such factors as sales, assets, earnings, products or services, markets, and management. If the intrinsic value is less than market price, fundamental analysts recommend sale. Alternatively, if the intrinsic value is greater than the market price, those analysts recommend purchase.

Fundamental analysis places considerable reliance upon financial statements, which technical analysts usually ignore. Most technical analysts believe that attempts to measure intrinsic value are futile as well as time-consuming. Technicians do not need to look for new information because that information is reflected in price movements. Changes in demand and supply are quickly reflected in prices.

The key to investment success is to detect trends early enough to benefit from the movement of prices. For example, price increases tend to be followed by further increases. Technical analysts claim that fundamental analysts are tardy in exploiting trends in prices because of the time they must spend in seeking, processing, and evaluating new financial information.

Technical indicators. There are numerous technical rules and techniques used to predict prices. Technical analysis frequently can be an arcane art so that evaluating some of the tools is nearly impossible because the interpretation is so subjective. This section discusses several of the techniques that are widely publicized and can be interpreted objectively.

Advances versus declines. This figure is a measure of the number of securities that have advanced each day and the number of securities that have declined. Many newspapers publish the number of advances and declines each day on the various markets. The ratio of advances to declines provides a better indication of the trend of the overall market than an index like the Dow Jones Industrial Average (DJIA), which is composed of only 30 stocks, or even the S&P 500.

The breadth of the market is considered particularly important at peaks and troughs. Technicians believe that the market may be near its peak if the DJIA is increasing while the ratio of advances to declines is decreasing. The market may be nearing a trough when the DJIA is declining and the ratio of advances to declines is increasing.

Moving-average analysis. According to technicians, this analysis provides a way of detecting trends in stock prices. A moving average is periodically computed by dropping the earliest number and adding in the most recent number. For example, a 200-day moving average is calculated by adding the most recent day's price to the closing prices of the previous 199 days and dividing by 200. The computation of a moving average tends to eliminate the effect of short-term fluctuations and provides a standard against which to compare short-term fluctuations. For example, technicians consider a downward penetration through a moving-average line as a signal to sell, particularly when a moving-average price is flattening out. On the other hand, analysts are bullish about a stock when the graph of a moving-average price flattens out and the stock's price rises through the moving average.

Sentiment indicators. There are several indicators that attempt to measure investors' attitudes toward the stock market. Some sentiment indicators measure investors' attitude directly, whereas others track the recommendations of investment advisers. Technical analysts look at this data differently than what might be expected. When investors are extremely bullish, technical analysts regard the market as vulnerable. When investors are very bearish, they regard this as a buying opportunity. Technical analysts justify this belief by noting that investors become more and more bullish as the market rises, until they have used up their cash. With the reduction in cash available to investors, the demand factor slackens and the market has nowhere to go but down. *Investors Intelligence* polls investment advisers weekly and the results are published in both *Barron's* and *Investor's Business Daily*. The market is regarded as nearing a top when 60% of the investment advisers are bullish. When less than 20% of the advisers are bullish, the market may be approaching a bottom.

Evaluating technical analysis. No technical indicator has proven to be an infallible predictor of future stock prices. There is no sure and easy road to stock market riches. Technical analysis may be useful for some investors. However, other investors should not feel at a disadvantage if they do not use technical analysis in trading stocks.

The investors who have been most successful are those who have pursued a sound investment strategy geared to making profits over the long term. For those investors who want to learn more about technical analysis, John J. Murphy's *Technical Analysis of the Financial Markets: A Comprehensive Guide to Trading Methods and Applications* (New York Institute of Finance, 1999) is a useful guide. Newsletters such as *The Chartist* and *Market Logic* make predictions based upon technical indicators. An invaluable source of data for technical analysis is *Barron's*.

The best source on the Web for charts of stock movements and other technical data is *www.bigcharts.com*. For some excellent free tutorials on technical analysis, see *www.equityanalytics.com*.

23

INVESTMENT NEWSLETTERS AND ADVISERS

Newsletters are reports issued to subscribers that purport to time the markets, describing exactly the right time to buy or sell securities. More than a million investors subscribe to hundreds of newsletters, paying anywhere from $50 to over $2000 per year for advice that varies widely in quality and usefulness. Many investment newsletters make extravagant claims about the performance of their recommendations and suggest that following their advice will lead to stock market riches. Investors should be wary of that kind of flamboyant claim, which is found in some advertisements. However, some of the newsletters can be useful in enhancing the performance of an investor's stock portfolio.

The various services reflect nearly every approach to investing. Many of them make recommendations based upon technical analysis, which attempts to predict future prices based upon the pattern of past prices (see Key 22). Other services employ a fundamental approach—analyzing earnings, cash flows, asset values, and other basic financial data. Services with this latter approach include two of the largest investment advisory firms:

1. *Value Line Investment Survey*
2. *The Outlook*, by Standard & Poor's

Other advisory services are more specialized, focusing on small stocks, stock options, stock charts, insider trading, mutual funds, or other particular areas of investment. Newsletter writers do not have to pass an exam or meet qualifications of any kind. Anyone can publish an investment newsletter and sell it to the investing public.

Evaluating newsletters. Most investors do not have the time or the financial resources to evaluate all the newsletters available. Fortunately, resources exist to provide assistance. Each month, Mark Hulbert publishes *The Hulbert Financial Digest* (703-750-9060), which evaluates the performance of more than 160 investment newsletters. Hulbert describes each service in detail and evaluates the quality and effectiveness of each newsletter's recommendations according to a number of objective criteria. Hulbert also writes a column that appears every other Sunday in *The New York Times*, which discusses the newsletter industry.

From year to year, the performance success of newsletters changes. Only a minority consistently has provided superior investment performance. The five newsletters that have the highest return during the past decade according to Hulbert are as follows:

- *OTC Insight*
- *Timer Digest*
- *MPT Review*
- *New Issues*
- *The Chartist*

An inexpensive way to become familiar with some of the services is to take advantage of the sample offer made by *Select Information Exchange* (212-247-7123), which provides trial subscriptions to four services in its catalog for $69.

24

OTHER SOURCES
OF INFORMATION

The purpose of this Key is to describe the primary sources of information available to assist individuals in making investment decisions. An investor does not need to read all of the sources to make an informed choice. However, it is necessary to be aware of trends in the economy and business activity. Most successful investors have a broad knowledge of the business and investment environment, so that they are capable of making judgments independent of the so-called experts. Such knowledge is important because the opinions of experts frequently are contradictory.

The most accessible source of information for nearly all investors is the financial section of a newspaper. Newspapers vary from excellent to poor in their coverage of financial developments. Both *The New York Times* and *Washington Post* have excellent financial sections and are widely available. Many investors also have chosen to supplement their local newspapers with a specialized financial newspaper, such as *The Wall Street Journal,* by far the most widely read daily of its type. *Investor's Business Daily* also is useful, particularly to those investors who use technical analysis.

There also are many general business periodicals and financial magazines available. *Business Week, Fortune,* and *Forbes* are three major business magazines. *Business Week* is oriented toward news reporting. In contrast, *Forbes* and *Fortune* (both published biweekly) focus on specific companies and business personalities. *Fortune* has greatly improved its coverage of investing topics in recent years. Investors should examine these periodicals and subscribe to at least one that appears most useful in enhancing their understanding of the stock market. *Barron's,* the weekly sister publication to *The Wall Street Journal,* provides a wealth of useful financial data as well as columns and features on events significant to investors. *Money* carries many articles on investments and also is a useful source of information on all aspects of financial planning.

Statistical services. Standard & Poor's (S&P) provides a broad array of products covering the entire investment arena. With respect to stocks, S&P publishes a monthly *Stock Guide*, the weekly *Outlook,* and a series of individual stock reports available at brokerage firms. These one-page reports provide a useful summary and description of a company's operations and financial history.

S&P has an excellent personal investment Web site called PersonalWealth.com (*www.personalwealth.com*). The monthly Web site subscription of $9.95 includes 20 *Enhanced Analytics* per month, or they may be purchased on line for $1 each.

Another excellent advisory service is the *Value Line Investment Survey,* a publication providing a one-page summary of useful financial data on individual companies. It also provides separate rankings on a 1–5 scale of timeliness and safety. *Timeliness* is the probable price performance relative to the market over the upcoming 12 months. *Safety* is the stock's future price stability and the company's current financial strength, where a rank of 1 is the highest. This systematized approach tells the investor exactly how *Value Line* regards the prospects of each company. (Descriptions of other advisory services are discussed in Key 23.)

Direct from the company. Before buying stock in a company, an investor should gather all the information he or she can from the company itself. The phone number can be found by checking the company's Web site or a Web site like Yahoo!Finance (*www.quote.yahoo.com*)—click the "profile" button for a telephone number. In response to phone queries, shareholder relations will send an annual report, Form 10-Q, and a proxy statement upon request. The contact person typically will direct the caller to the company's Web site as well.

The *annual report* is the formal report issued yearly by a corporation to its stockholders. It includes the president's letter, management's discussion and analysis of operations, balance sheet, income statement, statement of cash flows, note disclosures, and the report of the independent auditors.

Form 10-Q is a quarterly update to the annual report. It contains condensed financial information that updates the company's financial position and results of operations for the quarter.

The *proxy statement* provides information about items to be voted upon at the annual meeting. In addition, it provides information about management and directors not available in other reports to stockholders. Of particular interest is the number of shares owned by officers and directors. This data is important because, in general, the greater their ownership of common stock, the more likely that their interests are aligned with those of the stockholders.

Companies must transmit a Form 10-K (very similar to the annual report), Form 10-Q, and proxy statement to the SEC. The SEC makes those forms available on its Web site (*www.sec.gov/edgarhp.htm*), which unfortunately is not very user-friendly. A better way to tap into this information is to use the Web site called FreeEdgar (*www.freeedgar.com*).

25

MARKET TIMING

Is this a good time to buy or sell stocks? Two basic approaches exist to the timing question: (1) market timing and (2) buy-and-hold. A market timing approach involves selling stocks when a downturn is anticipated and buying stocks when the market begins to head upward. Buy-and-hold means that the portion of the portfolio allocated to stocks is fully invested in the stock market at all times. In other words, while an investor may buy and sell individual stocks, he or she remains fully invested in the stock market. If the up-and-down movements of the market could be anticipated, then returns could be increased. There is no evidence that market upturns and downturns can be predicted with enough accuracy to compensate for the increased transaction costs and adverse tax consequences, however.

Using technical analysis to time the market is particularly dangerous (Key 22). The market historically has gone up in two out of every three years. The investor who converts his or her stocks to cash is very likely to be out of the market when it is rallying.

In the 1980s, the Standard & Poor's (S&P) 500 Stock Index climbed an average of 17.6%. However, an investor who missed the best 10 days of the decade (out of a total of 2,528 trading days), increased his or her portfolio by only 12.6%. This experience has been repeated in the 1990s. The lesson is that it is very difficult, if not impossible, to anticipate the infrequent large spurts in the market that are so critical to long-term performance.

If an investor recognizes the difficulty of timing the market—and still would like to periodically reshape his or her portfolio—then consider recent stock market performance. Since 1926, the S&P 500 Stock Index has returned an average of 11.2%. Since 1950, the annual return has been 12.5%. In the ten years from 1989 to 1998, the average annual compound return was a startling 19.2%, way above the long-run average performance of the market.

The first lesson is very simple. The 1990s were an unusual period in terms of stock market performance. It is highly unlikely that stock returns in the next decade will equal those of the previous one. Further, in the last 75 years, we have experienced 40 declines of 10% or more in the market. Of those 40 declines, 10 averaged a terrifying 33%. The second lesson is indisputable: there will be market convulsions in the future.

Having cited these cautionary statistics, it is important to recognize that common stocks have provided an average after-inflation rate of return of about 7% per year over the period from 1802 to the present. This performance easily trumps that of either bonds or cash equivalents.

In the long-run, stock prices are determined by two fundamental factors: (1) expected earnings and (2) interest rates. Corporate earnings historically have increased at an average of 7% to 8% per year. There is no reason to believe that this growth will not be repeated in the future, although the growth each year can vary substantially. The future course of interest rates is unknowable. However, higher interest rates make fixed-income securities more attractive than stocks. The converse is also true.

Presidential election cycle. An interesting indicator is based upon the presidential election cycle. Every four years, stock prices tend to perform much better in the last two years of an administration than in the first two years. This difference arises because the incumbent President acts to ensure the party's return to power in years three and four.

Yale Hirsch has extensively researched the presidential election cycle, with the results providing evidence of the validity of this indicator (see Exhibit 4). Note that the sum of the election year and pre-election year of the 42 administrations since 1832 produced a total net market gain of 703.2% (see shaded columns of Exhibit 4), far in excess of the 251.8% gain of the sum of the first two years of these administrations. Although the evidence is convincing, there have been misleading signals. For example, the Clinton years witnessed excellent post-election returns despite the prediction of this indicator.

An update of the presidential election cycle is provided annually in Yale Hirsch's *Stock Trader's Almanac* (The Hirsch Organization Inc., 184 Central Avenue, Old Tappan, New Jersey 07675). This publication contains a wealth of information useful to investors.

EXHIBIT 4
Presidential Election/Stock Market Cycle
Stock Market Action Since 1832
Annual % Change in Dow Jones Industrial Average

4-Year Cycle Beginning	Election Year	President Elected	Post-Election Year	Midterm Year	Pre-Election Year
1832	4.8%	Jackson (D)	-0.9%	13.0%	3.1%
1836	-11.7	Van Buren (D)	-11.5	1.6	-12.3
1840*	5.5	W.H. Harrison (W)**	-13.3	-18.1	45.0
1844*	15.5	Polk (D)	8.1	-14.5	1.2
1848*	-3.6	Taylor (W)**	0.0	18.7	-3.2
1852*	19.6	Pierce(D)	-12.7	-30.2	1.5
1856	4.4	Buchanan (D)	-31.0	14.3	-10.7
1860*	14.0	Lincoln (R)	-1.8	55.4	38.0
1864	6.4	Lincoln (R)**	-8.5	3.6	1.6
1868	10.8	Grant (R)	1.7	5.6	7.3
1872	6.8	Grant (R)	-12.7	2.8	-4.1
1876	-17.9	Hayes (R)	-9.4	6.1	43.0
1880	18.7	Garfield (R)**	3.0	-2.9	-8.5
1884*	-18.8	Cleveland (D)	20.1	12.4	-8.4
1888*	4.8	B. Harrison (R)	5.5	-14.1	17.6
1892*	-6.6	Cleveland (D)	-24.6	-0.6	2.3
1896*	-1.7	McKinley (R)	21.6	22.5	9.2
1900	7.0	McKinley (R)**	-8.7	-0.4	-23.6
1904	41.7	T. Roosevelt (R)	38.2	-1.9	-37.7

(continued)

82

EXHIBIT 4 (continued)

Presidential Election/Stock Market Cycle
Stock Market Action Since 1832
Annual % Change in Dow Jones Industrial Average

4-Year Cycle Beginning	Election Year	President Elected	Post Election Year	Midterm Year	Pre-Election Year
1908	46.6	Taft (R)	15.0	-18.0	0.5
1912*	7.6	Wilson (D)	-10.3	-5.1	81.7
1916	-4.2	Wilson (D)	-21.7	10.5	30.5
1920*	-32.9	Harding (R)**	12.7	21.7	-3.3
1924	26.2	Coolidge (R)	30.0	0.3	28.8
1928	48.2	Hoover (R)	-17.2	-33.8	-52.7
1932*	-23.1	F. Roosevelt (D)	66.7	4.1	38.5
1936	24.8	F. Roosevelt (D)	-32.8	28.1	-2.9
1940	-12.7	F. Roosevelt (D)	-15.4	7.6	13.8
1944	12.1	F. Roosevelt (D)**	26.6	-8.1	2.2
1948	-2.1	Truman (D)	12.9	17.6	14.4
1952*	8.4	Eisenhower (R)	-3.8	44.0	20.8
1956	2.3	Eisenhower (R)	-12.8	34.0	16.4
1960*	-9.3	Kennedy (D)**	18.7	-10.8	17.0
1964	14.6	Johnson (D)	10.9	-18.9	15.2
1968*	4.3	Nixon (R)	-15.2	4.8	6.1
1972	14.6	Nixon (R)***	-16.6	-27.6	38.3
1976*	17.9	Carter (D)	-17.3	-3.1	4.2
1980*	14.9	Reagan (R)	-9.2	19.6	20.3
1984	-3.7	Reagan (R)	27.7	22.6	2.3
1988	11.8	Bush (R)	27.0	-4.3	20.3
1992*	4.2	Clinton (D)	13.7	2.1	33.5
1996	26.0	Clinton (D)	22.6	16.1	
%Gain	296.2%		75.1%	176.7%	407.0%
#Up	29		19	25	30
#Down	13		22	17	11

*Party in power ousted **Death in office ***Resigned

D—Democrat, W—Whig, R—Republican

Based on annual close. Prior to 1886 based on Cowles and other indices.

Source: Reprinted with permission from *Stock Trader's Almanac* by Yale Hirsch, The Hirsch Organization Inc., 2000, p. 139.

26

MARKET EFFICIENCY

After the stock market crash of October 19, 1987, when the Dow Jones Industrial Average plunged a record 22.6%, articles in *Forbes, Fortune,* and other publications discussed the efficient market hypothesis (EMH) and the insight it offered into reasons for the decline. Although the EMH has been a topic of academic interest and debate for the past 35 years, it has only recently received the attention of the financial press.

Market efficiency is a description of how prices in competitive markets react to new information. An efficient market is one in which prices adjust rapidly to new information and in which current prices fully reflect all publicly available information. Thus, according to EMH, an investor cannot use publicly available information to earn above average profit (profits that exceed a buy-and-hold strategy). Market prices already reflect public information contained in balance sheets, income statements, dividend declarations, and so forth. According to this theory, then, neither fundamental nor technical analysis can produce investment recommendations that will earn above average profits (see Keys 13 and 22).

Evidence. Although the EMH provides important lessons for investors, its followers frequently tend to overstate their case. A couple of points should be emphasized. First, although much empirical evidence supports the EMH, several strategies have been able to beat the market consistently and thus seem to be exceptions to the market's efficiency. A market, rather than being perfectly efficient or inefficient, is *more or less* efficient. Efficiency is a function of how closely a market is followed. The case for the efficiency of stock prices on the New York Stock Exchange (NYSE) is undoubtedly stronger than for those in the over-the-counter market because the latter stocks are not monitored to the same extent as stocks listed on the NYSE.

Second, market efficiency varies depending upon the qualifications of investors. For the majority of investors, the market is an efficient mechanism. However, there are investors who consistently generate above-average returns. This performance by a minority of investors should not obscure the fact that all the evidence, including the performance of mutual funds and the recommendations of investment newsletters, indicates that it is very difficult to earn above-average profits on a consistent basis. The EMH is therefore an aggregate concept applying to the majority of investors or the market as a whole.

Lessons of the EMH. Although many analysts are dubious about the EMH, it provides three important lessons that should be observed by all investors:

1. Tips are rarely of value. The market processes new information very quickly.
2. A portfolio should not be churned. A strategy that involves frequent purchases and sales of stocks is likely to be a loser because the commission costs eat up any profits an investor makes.
3. It is not easy to beat the market; only a small minority of investors consistently do so. High returns usually can be achieved only through assuming greater risk. However, greater risk raises the possibility of increased losses as well as gains.

27

MERGERS AND ACQUISITIONS

A merger is a combination of two or more companies. There are many different ways to effect a merger, or business combination. Basically, it involves either a stock acquisition, an asset acquisition, or a combination of the two. In a stock acquisition, the acquiring company obtains controlling interest in the voting stock of the acquired company and "absorbs" it. In an asset acquisition, the acquiring company directly purchases the assets of the acquired company. "Merger" often is combined with "acquisitions" and abbreviated as M&A. When "takeover" is used in the context of M&As, it implies that the acquired company's management opposed the acquisition.

Tender offer. A tender offer is an offer to all stockholders of a company to purchase shares. The offer specifies number of shares, price, and time frame in which the offer is good. The offer may come from the company itself or from another company or investor group. A tender offer made to current stockholders by an outsider typically is part of a hostile takeover. Usually the offer to buy is open only for a period of up to several weeks. All stockholders have the option to sell or "tender" any or all shares that they own. The tender offer price usually is substantially above the current price to encourage stockholders to sell. The stock price will increase in response to the tender offer, but will settle at a level slightly below the tender offer price. This gap arises because of a possibility that the takeover will fail.

Takeover terminology. Takeover mania has spawned a colorful vocabulary used in the financial news. Many of these terms describe the efforts of companies to fend off corporate raiders.

• *Poison pill.* A tactic used by corporations to defend against unfriendly takeovers by making them more expensive to the acquiring company. For example, preferred stock is sometimes issued to give stockholders the right to redeem it at an extravagant premium after a takeover.

• *White knight.* A person or corporation that saves a company from a hostile takeover by taking it over on terms more favorable to the acquired company. The white knight is considered more suitable by the target company and often is courted by the target company to make an offer.

• *Golden parachute.* Executives concerned about their positions guarantee themselves lucrative severance pay or stock allowances in the event of a takeover.

• *Greenmail.* Greenmail is a concept similar to blackmail, although not illegal. It refers to a corporation buying a block of its own stock owned by a potential acquirer at a price that substantially exceeds the market price. Management thus pays a premium to take the stock out of the hands of an unfriendly corporate raider.

• *Shark repellent.* A potential takeover target may try to enhance its defenses by the inclusion of corporate bylaws designed to put obstacles in the path of a takeover company.

• *Pacman defense.* The target company attempts to counteract a takeover bid, which is accomplished by buying the acquirer's stock as a threat to taking it over.

Mergers and acquisitions are occurring at a record pace as we enter the new millennium. In 1998, companies announced $2.5 trillion in mergers and acquisitions worldwide, the fourth consecutive record year, up from $1.6 trillion a year earlier. The number of mergers should continue to rise as companies unite to cut costs and compete worldwide. The creation of a single currency in Europe also will create the need for giant companies that can serve a market as large as that of the United States.

28

FINANCIAL LEVERAGE

Financial leverage is the use of debt to magnify returns. Speculators attempt to multiply returns by supplementing their own funds with borrowed funds. A margin account can be established to use leverage to invest in stocks and other securities. Under current rules, the initial requirement for margin on stocks is 50%. Therefore, to purchase $20,000 worth of stock, an investor must put up $10,000 in cash. The remainder can be borrowed from the brokerage firm. Of course, leverage is a two-way street because it magnifies losses as well as gains.

Companies use leverage to increase income. Like individuals, they use debt to increase the resources available to generate future profits. Leveraging is successful as long as the money borrowed produces returns greater than the interest charges on the additional debt incurred. However, debt involves risk because a company commits itself to making fixed interest payments. A company that does not meet its interest payments generally becomes insolvent. Financial leverage is illustrated with the following example.

Assume ABC Corporation has $1,000,000 in total assets, and its capital structure (liabilities plus stockholders' equity) consists of 60% debt and 40% equity:

Assets	$1,000,000
Liabilities	$ 600,000
Stockholders' Equity	$ 400,000

The cost of debt is 10% and the average tax rate is 40%. If ABC Corporation earns $200,000 in income, the return on stockholders' equity is 21%, computed as follows:

Operating income	$200,000
Less: Interest expense	60,000
Income before tax	140,000
Less: Income tax expense	56,000
Net income	$84,000

$$\frac{\text{Net income}}{\text{Stockholders' equity}} = \frac{\$84,000}{\$400,000} = 21\%$$

If ABC Corporation increases net income by 20% to $240,000, the return on stockholders' equity increases from 21% to 27%, a 29% increase:

Operating income	$240,000
Less: Interest expense	60,000
Income before tax	180,000
Less: Income tax expense	72,000
Net income	$108,000

$$\frac{\text{Net income}}{\text{Stockholders' equity}} = \frac{\$108,000}{\$400,000} = 27\%$$

In other words, a 20% increase in income produces a 29% increase in stockholders' equity. In this case, leverage works for the stockholders. Interest is a fixed charge, and the income generated by using debt in excess of the interest charges accrues to the benefit of stockholders.

Conversely, leverage can harm stockholders. Assume that ABC Corporation's income drops by 20% to $160,000 and the return on equity drops from 21% to 15%, a decrease of 29%:

Operating income	$160,000
Less: Interest expense	60,000
Income before tax	100,000
Less: Income tax expense	40,000
Net income	$60,000

$$\frac{\text{Net income}}{\text{Stockholders' equity}} = \frac{\$60,000}{\$400,000} = 15\%$$

In this case, a 20% decrease reduces the return on stockholders' equity by 29%, illustrating that incurring debt creates opportunities *and* additional risk. Highly leveraged companies can be risky investments, particularly when a downturn in the economy occurs.

29

INVESTMENT BANKING

Investment bankers are firms that specialize in assisting companies and governments in marketing a new debt or equity security issue to pay for capital expenditures like buildings and machinery. The term "investment banker" can be misleading, however. For one thing, investment banks do not accept deposits or make loans, as do other banks. Nor do they permanently invest their own funds in the securities they issue. Rather, their general function is to purchase new issues of stocks and bonds from corporations and governments and to arrange for the sale of those securities to the investing public. The sale of new securities to raise funds is a *primary market* transaction. In their early years, investment banks operated principally in the primary market. More recently, most of their revenues have been derived from trading in the secondary market. After a new issue of stocks or bonds is sold in the primary market, subsequent trades of the securities take place in the secondary market.

Functions of investment bankers. When bringing an issue to the primary market, an investment banker typically provides the client company with four basic services:

1. *Advisement.* Initially, the investment banker will serve in an advisory capacity. When a company or government decides to raise capital, the investment banker offers advice on the amount of funds needed and the available means of raising it. Specifically, the investment banker will assist the issuer in making the determination as to the general characteris-

91

tics of the issue and the price and timing of the offering. In addition, the investment banker may assist clients in analyzing mergers, acquisitions, and refinancing of operations.

2. *Administration.* After the decision to issue the securities is made, the investment banker helps the client company complete the paperwork and satisfy legal requirements. Of primary importance is the registration statement that must be filed with the Securities and Exchange Commission (SEC) before each interstate security offering (see Key 5).

   Most of the information contained in the registration statement also is included in the prospectus. This document must be distributed to every investor who is considering the purchase of the new security. It contains information about the issuer's financial condition, management, business activities, planned use of the funds, and a description of the securities to be issued. Many investors have trouble understanding a prospectus because of the legal language. Thus, it is sometimes necessary to seek professional assistance to fully understand a prospectus.

3. *Risk bearing.* Investment bankers generally agree to buy all of a corporation's new securities at a specified price. Then they resell those securities in small units to individual and institutional investors. This process is referred to as *underwriting.* The underwriting process involves risk because of the time interval between purchase by the investment banker and sale of the securities to the investors. During this interval, market conditions may deteriorate, forcing the investment banker to sell the securities at a loss.

   If the issuance is too large for a single investment banker to handle, it can form a temporary partnership with other investment banks. Such partnerships are called syndicates. The advantage of a syndicate is that it spreads the risk of loss over all of the investment banks in the group.

4. *Distribution.* The distribution service involves the marketing or sale of the securities after they are purchased from the issuer. Once the syndicate receives the securities, members are allocated their portion of the securities to sell at the predetermined price. Investment bankers earn income by selling the security at a price that exceeds what they paid—this difference is known as the *spread.* The selling costs for common stock are much greater than those incurred for selling bonds. Bonds are sold in large blocks to a few large institutional investors, whereas common stock usually is sold to large numbers of individual and/or institutional investors.

Investment bankers do not confine their activities to the primary market. They also play an important role in the secondary market. As dealers, investment bankers buy and sell securities in which they specialize. Investment bankers also are involved in trading large blocks of securities among institutional investors. Further, they redistribute large blocks of securities to individuals and institutions through secondary offerings.

30

INITIAL PUBLIC OFFERINGS (IPOs)

Planet Hollywood, with its ownership consisting of glamorous movie stars, was a hot IPO in 1996. Shares of the restaurant chain shot up from $18 for each share to as high as $32⅛ before closing at $26⅞ the first day of trading. Three years and many financial disappointments later, Planet Hollywood was bankrupt.

Internet stocks dominated the 1999 IPO market. Few investors were able to buy stock at the offering price but that did not stop them from jumping in after the first trades. *TheStreet.com* jumped on May 11, 1999 from $19 to as high as $71.25 on its first day. Based on its closing price of $60, *TheStreet.com*'s market capitalization (share price times number of shares outstanding) equaled $1.6 billion—an astounding amount for a company that had revenue of just $4.6 million and a loss of $16.4 million in 1998, its third consecutive year of losses. Within three weeks, its price per share had dropped to less than $30 per share.

Wall Street syndicate managers estimate that institutions get to buy about 60% of the typical IPO deal and 80% of the hot deals. In a normal deal, individuals might get allocated 25% of the shares, whereas in an exciting offering they might be lucky to get 5% of the shares. After the institutions rake in their shares, there is not much left to divvy up among individuals. Unfortunately, the way the system works is that the easiest offerings for individuals to participate in are those the institutions do not want to touch. These offerings often are of dubious quality.

What has been the long-term performance of IPOs? The answer is simply, *not good*. A study by Joy Ritter, professor of finance at the University of Illinois, found the average return to be only 5% per year. A more recent study of 3200 IPOs since 1994 found that by 1999, 30% now traded below their offering price and many had barely moved since their first-day performance. IPOs do reasonably well after the first quarter, but after the first year the return often becomes negative. Robert Natale, former editor of Standard & Poor's *Emerging & Special Situations* newsletter, has long asserted that IPOs underperform the market in the long term, whether in a bull or bear market. He normally recommends that IPOs be held no longer than three months after the offering. For those able to get in at the offering price, he recommends selling the shares quickly and moving the proceeds elsewhere. Although this strategy violates the axiom that most investors should buy for the long term, the IPO market is not for most small investors.

Why do IPOs underperform after a short time? Several possible answers exist. One reason has to do with SEC regulatory requirements. Company insiders are prohibited from selling their shares during a period subsequent to the offering date (usually 3–6 months). Once the prohibition period has expired, insiders start selling and prices weaken. Another reason is that underwriters time the sale to coincide with peaks in the market and industry cycles. Thereafter, the company's stock does not seem as attractive.

Investors who are determined to find another Microsoft, which soared more than twentyfold in value within five years after its IPO in 1986, can improve chances of success by following several guidelines:

1. Look at the P/E ratio. A common gauge of value is the price of a stock divided by its per-share earnings for the past 12 months. This information is presented in the prospectus that is give to prospective buyers of the offering. This ratio should be

comparable to other companies in the same industry. We do not recommend buying stocks in companies that do not generate earnings and have little prospect of producing profits in the future.

2. Look for a sustained rate of growth in earnings per share for at least three years, rather than a mediocre record with one big year preceding the offering.

3. Check a company's profit margins before tax and interest. Stable or rising margins are preferable; falling or cyclical margins are a red flag to avoid the IPO.

4. Review the prospectus for any significant problems. They should be described in a section labeled "risk factors." Watch for such items as major disputes with the IRS about unpaid taxes, toxic-waste liabilities, or antitrust suits.

5. Note the use of the proceeds from the sale. It is positive if the money is going to be used for expansion or to pay off debt. What is suspicious is when the company's main owners are cashing out by reducing their own stock holdings.

6. Evaluate the quality of the underwriter. Some underwriters have reasonably good long-term records in pricing IPOs and supporting them in subsequent trading. Others have dumped a lot of losers on the market. Examining an underwriter's recent offerings can be a clue about the success of the new issue.

31

ARBITRAGE

The law of one price is an economic principle stating that at any given moment, identical goods should sell at identical prices everywhere in the world. A share of General Motors common stock should sell for the same price in the United States as it does in Europe. If these shares do not sell for the same price in both markets, arbitrage actions will occur and the law of one price will prevail. Arbitrage is the simultaneous action of selling the higher priced of the two investments and buying the lower priced (to deliver against the sale), allowing the investor to earn a profit with no risk. The opportunity for arbitrage exists because of inefficiencies or differences in alternative markets for essentially the same asset. The individual exploiting these opportunities is known as an arbitrageur. Hedged or matched transactions differ from a price arbitrage transaction because they involve the simultaneous purchase and sale of similar, but not identical, assets with similar maturities.

Classic arbitrage. Classic arbitrage contributes to a fair, liquid, and efficient marketplace. As described above, the arbitrageur buys commodities or securities that are selling cheaply in one market and resells them in another market where the price is higher. Thus, the prices in all markets would tend to equalize. Classic arbitrage probably originated in international currency markets where, for example, an arbitrageur could buy a British pound that was selling for a lower price in London than in Amsterdam, and then make a profit by simultaneously selling the pound at the higher price.

Risk arbitrage. As international markets of securities and currencies developed, arbitrageurs expanded their activities to include transactions involving some risk. For example, if heavy selling of a currency occurs in New York, an arbitrageur might buy the currency with the expectation that he or she could sell it at a higher price in London the next day. This transaction involves risk, but it also carries the opportunity to make greater profits than typically occur under classic arbitrage. Theoretically, the marketplace benefits from the arbitrageur's activities because liquidity is added to the market by purchasing the currency when others are unwilling to do so.

Merger arbitrage. Merger arbitrage has become the dominant form of risk arbitrage. When two companies announce a merger or a single company announces a bid for another, an arbitrage opportunity is created. Generally, a discrepancy exists between the cash price of the securities involved and the price offered for the target company's stock. This discrepancy exists because of the risk that the deal may not be consummated. Also, a period of several months usually is involved between the time of announcement and transfer of ownership. An arbitrageur analyzes the difference between the offering price and current price, weighs the risks and rewards, and, if warranted, may bid up the price of the acquired company to a value thought to be appropriate. Again, the arbitrageur provides liquidity to the marketplace by buying securities from those investors who do not want the risk of waiting to see if the deal will be completed.

In 1999, with the pace of mergers and acquisitions at an all-time high, risk arbitrageurs were in high gear. The takeover boom has provided investment opportunities and has made it easier for them to raise money to make trades. Surprisingly, there is one door to arbitrage that is open to investors of more modest means. The no-load Merger fund (800-343-8959) is the only mutual fund dedicated to merger arbitrage, and the minimum investment is $2,000.

32

MARGIN TRADING

Trading on margin refers to the use of borrowed funds to supplement the investor's own money. The investor makes only partial payment for the securities and borrows the rest from a broker. Therefore, trading on margin is essentially trading on credit. The use of borrowed funds enables the investor to take a larger position in the stock market. Borrowing money to expand the opportunity for profits is called *leverage.*

Rules of margin trading. A margin account is simple to open. The investor signs a margin agreement and a securities loan consent form, which gives the broker permission to lend the securities in the investor's account (see the explanation of short selling in Key 33).

All securities purchased on margin are held in the name of a broker (*street name*) instead of the investor's name. However, the investor is the owner of the stock, reaping the profits and enduring the losses. In addition, investors are credited with all dividends received on these shares. Almost all stocks on the NYSE and AMEX and more than 2,000 over-the-counter securities can be traded on the margin. Three sets of rules govern margin trading:

1. The Federal Reserve Board's initial margin requirement as of this writing is 50%. This requirement means that the investor must pay a broker at least $5,000 in cash to purchase $10,000 in stock. If securities are deposited instead of cash, 50% of the current market value of the securities deposited may be used as margin.
2. Members of the NYSE are governed by stricter

requirements. The NYSE requires a minimum initial equity requirement of cash in the amount of $2,000 or its equivalent in securities to open a margin account. Therefore, on a purchase of $3,000, the investor must deposit $2,000, which is 66⅔% of $3,000, rather than the $1,500 required by the Fed.

3. In addition, the broker may require a higher initial margin than either the Fed's 50% requirement or the NYSE's $2,000 start-off minimum. For example, Charles Schwab requires a 70% margin on certain Internet stocks.

Example. Assume an investor purchased 500 shares of stock at $30 per share. In a regular cash account, the investor would have to pay $15,000 (500 × $30), plus commission. A margin account generally would enable the investor to deposit only 50% of the purchase price, or $7,500, plus commission. The broker lends the investor the remaining $7,500, on which the investor will be charged interest.

Maintenance of margin. After a margin account is opened, margin maintenance requirements become effective. The Fed has no regulations regarding margin maintenance, but the NYSE requires equity in the customer's account to be at least 25% of the market value of the securities held in the account. Individual member brokerage firms may require that the minimum equity percentage be somewhat higher than 25%.

If the value of an investor's securities drops below the required level, the broker will issue a margin call and the investor will have to provide more cash. Failing to do so generally results in the broker's liquidation of the investor's securities.

Undermargined accounts. An undermargined account is an account with a market value that is below minimum margin requirements. If the value of the investor's securities falls below this level, the investor will receive a margin call and must deposit additional cash or securities. If the investor is unable to make the required deposit in response to the call, the broker will sell sufficient securities from the investor's account to bring it up to the required minimum level.

For example, assume an investor purchased securities for $10,000 on margin by depositing $5,000 in cash. The minimum maintenance requirement is 25%. To determine if the 25% maintenance level is being approached, divide the amount of the debit balance (in this example, $5,000) by 3 and add the result to the debit balance. In this case, one third of $5,000 is $1666, plus the $5,000 debit balance equals $6,666. If the total value of the investor's stock declines to a point that is less than this amount, then the balance is undermargined by the difference.

Special margin requirements. Some special considerations include:

1. The NYSE can set special requirements on individual issues that show a combination of volume, price variation, or turnover of unusual dimensions to discourage undue speculation.
2. Margin rules now apply to some mutual funds.
3. Stock valued at less than $5 per share usually cannot be purchased on margin.

33

SHORT SALES

A short sale is the sale of a security that is not owned, with the intention of purchasing it later at a lower price. Most investors purchase stock with the expectation that a profit eventually will be made from a rise in the price of the stock. However, investors have an alternative way of generating a profit when they believe that a stock is overpriced and expect its price to decline. The strategy adopted in this case is to sell the stock short. The investor borrows the security from another investor through a broker and sells it in the market. Usually a broker has other clients who own the security, generally in a margin account, and are willing to loan shares (see Key 32).

An important aspect of a short sale order is that an investor does not receive the proceeds of the order at the time the trade is executed. In a short sale, the brokerage firm keeps the money until the short sale is covered; that is, the security is purchased. Further, to ensure that the short position will be covered in the event of a rise in the price of the stock, the broker requires the posting of collateral by the short seller.

A large short position in a stock is not necessarily a bearish or pessimistic indicator, according to many analysts. They theorize that a large pent-up demand exists for the stock by investors who ultimately will have to purchase it to pay back their borrowed stock. In such a case, a sudden buying rush is possible if the stock's price increases and investors cover their shorts and thus limit their losses. A large short interest can therefore be a signal that a stock's price will be volatile. Short-interest reports on stocks listed on the NYSE, AMEX, and NASDAQ are printed soon after the middle of each month in the financial press.

Technical points. First, a short sale can be made only on an uptick trade. In other words, a sale can occur only after an increase of ⅛ of a point or more in the stock's price. This restriction was implemented to prevent traders from forcing a profit on a short sale by continually selling short and thus pushing the price down. Second, a short seller is responsible for the dividends to the investor who loaned the stock. The purchaser of the stock sold short receives the dividend from the corporation. As a result, the short seller must pay the same amount to the investor who loaned the stock.

Risk of short selling. Short selling involves the ability to spot an overvalued stock. The price of a stock may seem too high, but the problem is that it is not possible to know how high the shorted shares can go. Many short sellers lose money not by being wrong, but by being early. A stock's price could go higher and higher, with the short sellers incurring larger and larger losses. When a stock is purchased, the price cannot go below zero. If a stock is shorted that is going up, the sky is the limit for the losses.

An excellent book to help with identifying prospects for shorting is *The Act of Short Selling* by Kathryn F. Staley (John Wiley & Sons, 1997).

34

DIAMONDS, SPIDERS, AND WEBS

In recent years, index funds, which are mutual funds that track a market index, have outperformed the great majority of actively managed mutual funds. As a result, money has poured into these funds making them the hottest sector of the mutual fund industry.

Index funds, however, do not offer the same trading flexibility as traditional common stocks. Mutual funds are bought or sold only at the end of the day when the net asset value is established. If an order is placed for a fund in the morning, what the net asset value will be at the end of the day is conjecture. Meanwhile, common stocks can be traded at any time during the trading day. For this reason, the AMEX created a series of exchange-listed index funds. These products combine many of the advantages of index funds with the superior trading flexibility of common stocks.

Spiders. In January 1993, the AMEX created an index product termed Standard & Poor's Depository Receipts—SPDRs, called *spiders.* The spider based on the S&P 500 Stock Index has the symbol "SPY" and holds shares of all the companies in the S&P 500, closely tracking the price performance and dividend yield of the index.

Spiders have become so popular that on most days they are the most actively traded listing on the AMEX. These investments enable investors to buy or sell the entire portfolio of the 500 huge companies making up the S&P 500 as easily as trading shares of stock. In addition, spiders also pay quarterly cash dividends representing dividends accumulated on the stocks of the S&P 500 held in trust, less fees and expenses. Finally, for those interested in investing in smaller companies, the AMEX has spiders that track the S&P 400 MidCap Index under the symbol MDY.

Webs. In 1996, the AMEX expanded its index offerings by launching Webs (World Equity Benchmark Shares), which are designed to give investors fast and economical access to international equity markets. Through a single security, investors can own a diversified foreign country stock portfolio that seeks to track the performance of a major benchmark index. Each Webs series represents an investment in a portfolio of publicly traded stocks in a selected country. Investment results are sought that correspond to the price and yield performance of a specific Morgan Stanley Capital International index (MSCI). MSCI indexes are leading country index benchmarks widely used by U.S. investors for their international investments.

Unlike American Depositary Receipts (ADRs) that provide an investment in just one company, shares of Webs offer targeted exposure to a portfolio of publicly traded foreign stocks in a selected country. Currently, Webs shares embrace 17 country-specific series of securities.

Diamonds. Diamonds (DIA) are exchange-traded funds that track the Dow Jones Industrial Average (DJIA), the most widely publicized of U.S. stock indexes. The DJIA consists of 30 giant companies with stocks that account for close to a quarter of the stock market's total value. Although professionals use the S&P 500 as their favorite benchmark, over longer periods the DJIA tracks the S&P 500 quite closely. Since the beginning of 1980 through the end of 1998, the Dow gained 13.4% a year, compared to 13.6% for the S&P 500.

Diamonds are very popular with individuals who use them as a simple tool for making broad bets on the direction of the market. Institutional investors have directed their attention much more to spiders.

NASDAQ-100 Index. The first product introduced after the combination of the NASDAQ and the AMEX in 1998 was in March 1999, based on the NASDAQ-100 Index (QQQ). This product is similar to spiders and diamonds in that it acts like an index fund, but tracks like a stock. These shares have been extremely popular because the NASDAQ is dominated by the stocks of companies in the high-technology industry, with growth that has been particularly explosive in the 1990s.

In summary, exchange-listed funds have been one of Wall Street's hottest products in the late 1990s. These intriguing investments certainly can have a place in a diversified portfolio. The brokerage commission will be an extra cost (compared to a no-load mutual fund), but investing in a fixed portfolio of securities not requiring expert stock pricing ensures low management fees. All these investments currently are listed on the AMEX. We would expect that to change and the choices to grow over the next decade.

35

ON-LINE INVESTING

How big is on-line investing? In 1995, it was a barely measurable percentage of transactions by individual investors. By the end of 1998, 25% of the transactions were handled on-line. More than 75% of the trades by Charles Schwab, the Internet's No. 1 broker, are on the Internet. Schwab is getting more than 70 million hits a day. Currently, there are more than 100 companies involved in on-line trading; on-line accounts are expected to double to 14 million in the period from 1999 to the end of 2000.

Price. The biggest advantage of on-line trading is the huge cost savings. On-line commissions are dramatically lower than those of full-service firms. Charles Schwab (*www.schwab.com*), which accounts for 27% of on-line trading, charges $29.95 per trade for up to 1000 shares and $0.03 per additional share. Other on-line brokers charge even less—Datek (*www.datek.com*) and Suretrade (*www.suretrade.com*) would charge less than $10.00 to trade 1000 shares. Buying 200 shares of a $20.00 stock costs $8.00 at Ameritrade (*www.Amer.trade.com*), $14.95 at E*Trade (*www.etrade.com*), $29.95 at Schwab, and $116.00 at a full-service firm. Full-service firms justify the extra cost they charge by the value of their advice and guidance supported by top research analysts. And it must be acknowledged that they still dominate the industry. The $420 billion in customer accounts in the on-line industry is still far exceeded by Merrill Lynch's $1.4 trillion. But the growth of the on-line industry far exceeds that of full-service firms and on-line trading will inevitably force radical change on the entire brokerage industry. Merrill Lynch confirmed this change when it announced that it would be offering on-line trading to all of its customers as of December 1, 1999.

Selection. With all the on-line brokers out there, it is not an easy task to select the one that is best suited to a specific investment style and objectives. Even the ratings of the best brokers conducted by various periodicals and services yield significantly different results. Forrester Research, for example, ranks Fidelity Investments, Datek, and Suretrade as the top three, whereas Barron's Online favors DLJ Direct, Discover, and National Discount Brokers.

Investors must conduct their own research. Cost alone should not be the deciding factor. Commissions charged by the on-line industry have recently leveled off, and on-line brokers increasingly are concentrating on improving the design of their Web sites, adding backup servers, enhancing capacity planning, and providing additional stock research. Several services are available to assist with the selection of an on-line broker:

- Expert Online Investment Advocates (*www.xolia. com*)
- Gomez Advisors' Internet Broker Scoreboard (*www.gomez.com*)
- Keynote Systems' Online Brokerage Index (*www.keynote.com*)
- The Motley Fool Brokerage Center (*www.fool.com*)

Execution. The burgeoning growth of on-line trading has caused its own set of problems. The SEC reports that complaints about on-line investing, including slow Web site response times, inadequate phone support, and problems getting trades executed soared 330% in 1998. Thousands of complaints involved annoyance at the slowdowns and interruptions in service that occur when market activity is hectic.

In 1999, several on-line firms had highly publicized breakdowns—periods during which no customer could make an on-line trade. Although these technical meltdowns are rare, investors might want to minimize the chance of an untimely disruption in the ability to trade. One possibility is to make sure that the broker provides reliable alternative methods of trading, such as dependable live call centers or branch offices. Schwab and Fidelity both qualify in this respect. Alternatively, many serious investors (those who trade at least once a month) have several on-line accounts to execute low-cost trades. The extra account serves as a backup in case of technical difficulties experienced by a broker. The additional advantage of having multiple accounts is that it provides access to a wider range of products, such as bonds or initial public offerings.

For active traders, quality of execution is the greatest concern. This criterion not only includes the whole process of placing orders, but also an evaluation of whether the broker has a well-organized trading screen that offers current real-time quotes, drop-down boxes to prevent data entry errors, and error checks that do not discourage trading. This appraisal is not easy. The services previously cited should help.

When market volume is heavy or when attempting to buy initial public offerings, it is wise to use limit orders rather than market orders even though they cost more. A limit order is a trade only at a specific price, whereas a market order will be executed at the current price. A limit order ensures that an investor will not be surprised by the price paid or received for a stock trade.

36

INDEX FUNDS

The hottest strategy in mutual fund investing is buying index funds. An index fund is simply a mutual fund with a portfolio designed to track a broad-based index, such as Standard & Poor's 500 Stock Index or the Wilshire 5000 Equity Index. Over the past three years, investors have poured money into these funds and currently about one quarter of the money invested in mutual funds is targeted to index funds. Vanguard Group's S&P Fund has been the best-selling fund in the United States for the last three years, and at $75 billion is now ranked second in total assets with the expectation of being first by the year 2000.

Performance. Why has indexing triumphed as a strategy for investing in mutual funds? The numbers tell the story. In 1998, the S&P 500 Stock Index outperformed 86% of all general equity funds. The year before that, it was 95%; in 1997, it was 75%. Over the decade ended December 1998, 85.7% of large-cap equity funds underperformed the S&P 500. Typically, a broad capitalization-weighted index can be expected to outperform about two thirds of the actively managed funds. Moreover, the evidence indicates that mutual fund managers who beat the index in one period are unlikely to beat the index in the next period. The past record of funds has not been a very good predictor of how they will do in the future.

Cost advantage. The biggest advantage of indexing and the primary reason for the difference in performance between active and passive investing is the substantially lower cost of index funds. Each dollar incurred in costs cuts the earnings of a fund by a dollar. Index funds are characterized by paltry expense ratios and minimal transaction costs, which translate into higher long-run performance. Vanguard's S&P 500 Fund has an expense ratio of 0.18%, way below the typical equity fund ratio of 1.45%. In addition, active managers replace an average of 87% of the stocks they own each year. This number is referred to as the fund's turnover rate. The turnover rate of an index fund is as low as 5%. Thus, actively managed funds normally incur far greater transaction costs than their indexed competitors. These trading costs for actively managed funds amount to 1.0%–1.35% of assets versus a typical 0.25% of assets for an index fund. Lower expense ratios and trading costs give index funds a 2.0%–2.5% cost advantage that is very difficult for actively managed funds to overcome.

Tax advantage. Because S&P 500 and Wilshire 5000 index funds have minimal portfolio turnover rates, taxable distributions are much lower. When an actively managed fund trades, it realizes capital gains. Active managers often run their funds with little regard for the tax consequences of trading. In good years, large gains often are realized and distributed to stockholders. In contrast, S&P 500 and Wilshire 5000 funds are highly tax efficient because they rarely sell securities.

Selection. The Vanguard Group (800-635-1511) pioneered index funds and have been by far the largest sellers of these funds to the individual investor. The Vanguard Group is known for its emphasis on minimizing costs, and no index fund should be picked that has an expense ratio exceeding 0.40%. Besides Vanguard, Fidelity Investments (800-544-8888), T. Rowe Price Associates (800-638-5560), and Charles Schwab (800-266-5623) all offer index funds.

With index funds, results are still dependent upon the vagaries of the market. But it still provides some level of comfort for investors to know they will not badly lag behind the averages.

The S&P 500 Stock Index has been dominated by

large capitalization (market price per share times the number of common shares outstanding) companies such as Microsoft, Dell, Cisco, and General Electric. Stocks of large-cap companies have performed particularly well over the last decade and have been a major factor in the stellar achievement of the S&P 500. Meanwhile, small-cap stocks have generally been in the doldrums. Investors who expect small-cap stock returns to improve relative to those of large-cap stock should use a total stock market fund as the core index holding.

Total stock market funds track the Wilshire 5000 Equity Index, which despite its name, includes about 7,200 domestic stocks with readily determinable prices. The Wilshire 5000 Equity Index comprises about 99% of the U.S. equity market, whereas the S&P 500 includes about 75%. Because the Wilshire 5000 Equity Index includes many small-cap stocks, it would reflect an improvement in the returns of the small-cap sector. John Bogle, chairman of the Vanguard Group, recommends this index as the best way to mimic the U.S. stock market. Incidentally, over the last five years, the Vanguard Total Stock Market fund has advanced an annual average of 21.6%, only modestly behind the 24.1% gain of Vanguard's S&P fund. The difference was caused by the lagging performance of stocks in the small-cap sector.

Other index funds. Although investors have readily accepted indexing to track U.S. markets, the same investors have been slow to embrace indexing overseas. Mutual fund managers have been able to convince investors that they can add value by stock picking because international stocks are not as closely followed. But in 1998, the international indexes easily outperformed the international funds, and investors' view of indexing internationally is starting to change.

Although international index products are fewer in number, two good choices are (1) the Vanguard Total International Stock Fund and (2) the Schwab International Index Fund. The Schwab Fund is more focused on developed countries and has gained an annual average of 8.5% over the last five years. Although this performance may seem unexciting, keep in mind that the international markets have badly underperformed the U.S. markets over the same period.

Indexing can be especially fruitful for those investors buying bonds to help cushion any downturn in the stock market. An intermediate-bond index fund is an especially good choice. Active managers can add little value in picking bonds, so minimizing expenses is even more critical than in selecting stocks. That is why the Vanguard Total Bond Market fund, with an expense ratio of 0.20%, is such a good choice. This fund has returned an average of 7.1% annually over the past five years and consistently ranks in the top 20% of its category.

37

FINANCIAL WEB SITES

Within the last five years, a stunning amount of information has become available to the individual investor. The Internet offers an immense amount of data that was available only to professionals just a few years ago. With more than 10,000 Web sites devoted to the topics of investing, the sheer volume of information can be intimidating and much of it has little value. However, there are numerous Web sites that can help investors make decisions. The selections included here have been found to be particularly useful.

Home base. Many Web sites are trying to be the first stop for stock research. However, a quick check of these financial "portals" discloses that much of the data originates from the same set of providers, such as Zack's and First Call for earnings estimates and Reuters for news. Because of the redundancy, choosing where to begin is a matter of personal preference.

Yahoo!Finance (*www.quote.yahoo.com*). Our current favorite starting point is Yahoo!Finance. With a clear, well-designed layout, Yahoo!Finance provides a wealth of answers obtainable with a single click. Along with delayed stock quotes (15 minutes for NASDAQ stocks, 20 minutes otherwise), Yahoo!Finance is a comprehensive news source that includes the following feeds: Reuters Financial News, PR Newswire, Standard & Poor's Business Wire, Zack's, company profiles, and mutual fund profiles. New feeds and services regularly are being added.

This Web site enables users to look up stock price and company news by ticker symbol; track a group of stocks with constantly up-to-date portfolio value; search all available news by keyword; browse news by specific industry; and choose to read each feed individually. Links to quotes, news, research, world markets, and other services such as *The Motley Fool, TheStreet.com*, and *Individual Investor* are available on the front page. The quote page includes links to charts, news, SEC filings, insider activity, fundamental data, analysts' opinions, and message boards. Incidentally, all this information is *free*.

Microsoft Investor (*www.investor.com*). This site has some unique features that previously cost $9.95 per month. In August 1999, Microsoft eliminated all charges, making this site one of the best values on the Internet. For those interested in news, it includes items from MSNBC and Reuters as well as Investor staff reports, which are updated three times daily. The Insight section has regular columnists who provide some of the best investment commentary on the Web. Want to buy a stock or fund? The Investor can screen 16,000 stocks and funds on more than 500 criteria to find just the right ones. They have also created 20 pre-set stock and fund screens to make getting started easy.

The Stocks section contains company profiles, customized price charts, and SEC filings, including a year's worth of quarterly financial filings plus annual filings, proxy statements, and other reports from the past four years. Those seeking assistance in formulating an investment strategy can look over the shoulders of six professional advisers managing portfolios on-line for Investor. After a portfolio of stocks and bonds has been selected, Investor provides current data, including market prices, news reports, and the portfolio's performance.

The Wall Street Journal Interactive Edition (*www.wsj.com*). Here is the way to have the leading business newspaper, *The Wall Street Journal*, continuously updated. The quality of the information accessible is what makes this Web site a standout. Subscribers are provided continuous news coverage, searchable archives, and access to detailed company data. Breaking news on topics and investments of the subscriber's choice are available. The section called Briefing Books provides an in-depth perspective on a company. These reports offer background, performance history, recent news, press releases, and many other details. Subscribers can even chart the company's stock performance by the criteria they deem most significant.

The *Interactive Edition* also provides access to *Barron's Online*, which includes recent editions of *Barron's* as well as in-depth market commentary. Also included is *SmartMoney Interactive*, which includes articles from the magazine *SmartMoney* as well as interactive tools and worksheets. One particularly neat feature of *SmartMoney* is the Sector Tracker section, which enables investors to track 122 market sectors and ten industry groups over five different time periods—and click for more information on individual stocks. The subscription price is a bargain at $49 per year($29 for print subscription to *The Wall Street Journal, Barron's,* or *SmartMoney*).

CBS *Market Watch (cbs.marketwatch.com).* CBS *Market Watch*, a joint venture between CBS and market information provider DBC, has a large staff providing original market news and commentary throughout the day. The Web site includes quotes, mutual fund data, charting, and portfolio tracking—at absolutely no cost.

FreeEdgar (*www.freeedgar.com*). All publicly traded companies have to submit a Form 10-K (annual report) and a Form 10-Q (quarterly report) to the Securities and Exchange Commission (SEC). This information is easier to access by using FreeEdgar rather than the SEC's Web site (*www.sec.gov*). Also, users can register to have E-mail alerts when their own companies file with the SEC.

TheStreet.com. This service was co-founded by Jim Cramer, the colorful and controversial hedge fund manager. He comments at least several times a day on market developments. At $9.95 a month, users get some of the finest journalism on the Web provided by an expert staff of writers.

Quicken.com (*www.quicken.com*). This great, all-purpose Web site includes stock market commentary, simple and useful search tools for stocks and funds, earnings estimates, and insider trading information. As the maker of the world's most popular investment software, Quicken has made this Web site user-friendly. The investment section includes not only stock and fund data, but also information on insurance, taxes, and retirement planning. Best of all, it's *free.*

The Motley Fool (*www.fool.com*). This Web site, created by the Gardner brothers, is dedicated to making investing easier. The Fool offers a 13-step program to educate beginning investors. Graduates are taught more sophisticated techniques, such as using screens to find fast-growing companies and tracking the latest favorites of the momentum followers. This free Web site also offers excellent summaries of the quarterly conference calls that major companies conduct with Wall Street analysts.

38

SMALL-CAP STOCKS

The market has had a prodigious climb in the last decade evidenced by the 19.19% annual increase in the S&P 500 in the period ending 1998. Yet those who look more closely at the data notice that not all segments of the market have participated equally. For example, the stocks of large-capitalization (large-cap) companies have considerably outperformed those of small-capitalization (small-cap) companies.

The market capitalization of a stock is equal to its share price times the number of shares outstanding. Large-cap stocks include such giants as Microsoft, General Electric, and IBM. Microsoft currently has the largest market capitalization of any company (over $400 billion). At the other end of the spectrum, we have the smaller-cap companies, which include the newly emerging companies.

What exactly is a small-cap stock? No definition is universally accepted, but market professionals generally categorize small-cap as less than $1 billion, large-cap as more than $4 billion, and mid-cap as between $1 and $4 billion. In any case, small-cap companies usually are significantly smaller than large-cap companies.

Small-cap returns. What makes smaller company stocks interesting investments are the long-run returns they have generated? Data from Ibbotson Associates shows that the average annual return from small-cap stocks over the period from 1926 to 1998 is 12.4%, which is 1.2% greater than that of large-cap stocks.

Looking at the data from a shorter investment horizon is even more instructive. There are 54 20-year holding periods from 1926 to 1998. In every one of those periods, stocks outgained bonds. More surprisingly, perhaps, small-cap stocks outgained large-cap stocks in 92% of those periods. For those interested in a shorter time horizon, the ten-year holding period results show small-cap stocks outperformed the large-cap stocks in 75% of the periods from 1926 to 1998.

It is important to keep these long-run results in mind because many investors have become disillusioned with small-cap stocks. Over the decade ending 1998, large-cap stocks have outperformed small-cap stocks in every single year.

Diversification. The returns of the last decade should not blind us as to the future potential of the small-cap sector. Clearly, the stocks included in the S&P 500 should form the core of every investor's U.S. stock portfolio. But small-cap stocks have risk and return characteristics that can help investors diversify their portfolios.

The way to reduce stock market risk is to invest in market sectors that are affected by different kinds of factors. When one segment of the market is weak, another might be less affected, reducing the effect of the weak segment. The combined effect of the two segments is to smooth the pattern of total returns. In other words, combining the two segments reduces the volatility of the portfolio, and volatility is a proxy for risk. There are periods where small-cap stock returns will exceed large-cap stock returns and vice versa. By diversifying and including both these segments in a portfolio, we should be able to reduce the fluctuation in returns on that portfolio.

Why not invest a large portion of investable resources in small-cap stocks? Although stocks of smaller companies have greater potential for long-term growth than larger or more mature companies, these stocks tend to be more volatile and riskier for the following reasons:

1. These companies are more prone to difficulties in economic downturns.
2. They usually do not pay dividends that can cushion a decline in stock values.

3. Because of fewer outstanding shares, these stocks are less liquid, making it more difficult at times to buy or sell shares.

Strategy. Our suggestion would be to devote no more than 10% to 20% of equity funds to small-cap stocks. If the small-cap allocation is boosted above 20%, the extra returns come with considerably enhanced risk. When liquidity dries up in a true bear market, small-cap stocks can get killed.

For those investors who insist on doing their own stock picking, we can suggest a simply strategy to assist in weaning out some possible candidates for purchases from the thousands available. Check *Investor's Business Daily*, which lists stocks' percentile scores for relative strength and earnings momentum. Pick out the stocks that rank in at least the 90th percentile in both categories. Then, combine those high scores with the best fundamentals. The Motley Fool (*www.fool.com*) has a tutorial on analyzing common stocks.

For investors who do not have enough time to research stock picks thoroughly or enough money to buy a sufficient number of stocks to spread risk, mutual funds are the best bet. Two good choices for those preferring index funds are (1) Vanguard SmallCap Index Fund (800-635-1511) and (2) Schwab SmallCap Index Fund (800-266-5623).

39

INSIDER TRADING

An insider typically is defined as a director, officer, or major stockholder of a corporation. The Securities and Exchange Commission (SEC) requires that the names of insiders be filed with the SEC. Subsequently, they must file reports for any month where there was any change in their holdings. The purpose of this requirement is to enable the SEC and stockholders to observe the actions of insiders to prevent abuses in the use of insider information to make profits by speculating in their own stocks. These insider reports are widely reported in the financial press.

Insiders are not prevented from trading in their own stocks. Rather, insider-trading sanctions are designed to prevent the misuse of confidential information not available to the general public. Some insiders buy and sell stocks to make personal profits; others relay information to friends or others who trade the stocks before the information is available to the general public.

Corporate insiders who trade their company's stocks must report all the details of the trade to the SEC (Form 144) on or before the tenth of the month following the trade. For example, an insider trade on January 5 must be reported by February 10. The SEC collects this information and releases it daily at its offices in Washington, D.C. In addition, the transaction reports are published monthly in the SEC Official Summary of Security Transactions and Holdings.

The Internet is the best source of information on insider activity. Both Yahoo!Finance (*www.quote.yahoo.com*) and Bloomberg (*www.bloomberg.com*) provide extensive disclosure on insider transactions. For those investors who want a more detailed analysis, InsiderTrader (*www.insidertrader.com*) costs $49 per year.

Using insider data. Logically, insiders should have superior knowledge of the real value of their company. Corporate insiders should be better informed about the company's current business activities and future prospects than either stockholders or security analysts. Although they cannot legally purchase stock based on material, nonpublic information, they can purchase stock upon their perception that the intrinsic worth of the stock exceeds the current market price.

A further legal provision limiting the rights of insiders to speculate in the stock of their own company has significant implications for investors. Any profit from the purchase or sale of the stock realized within a period of six months can be claimed by the company. A suit to recover this profit can be brought either by a stockholder or the issuing corporation. The purpose of this provision is to prevent insiders from using confidential information to speculate in the stocks of their companies.

Although several market forecasters use total insider activity to anticipate broad stock market movements (available in *Barron's* weekly), the relationship between total insider buying and selling and changes in the overall market is rather tenuous. For example, indicators of insider activity would be considered neutral to bullish prior to the crash of October 1987. However, insider data is a very useful clue about the prospects of an individual company. Several academic studies have found that stocks bought by insiders outperform the market.

Martin Zweig, a prominent investment adviser, defines an insider-buy signal as indicated when three or more insiders have bought and none have sold a stock within the most recent three-month period. Conversely, he defines an insider-sell signal as indicated when three or more insiders sell and none buy within that same period. Insider-sell signals are not as accurate as insider-buy signals because insiders may sell stocks for tax or other reasons not related to their perceptions of how well or how poorly their company is doing. Remember that insider trading has the most predictive value if it involves a substantial number of insiders and the number of shares traded is a substantial proportion of insiders' current holdings.

40

FOREIGN SECURITIES

As the world economy becomes increasingly interdependent, many investors are realizing the profits to be made by investing in foreign securities. With about half of the world's publicly traded stocks registered outside the United States, and with equity markets representing over half of the world's total capitalization, opportunities abound for the investor willing to expend the time and effort to analyze foreign markets. Do not be misled by the Asian market's meltdown in 1997 or the dismal performance of the Japanese market in the 1990s as compared to the United States. Although the U.S. market strongly outperformed foreign markets over the recent five years, this record was not typical. Over 24 years from 1969 to 1993, the Morgan Stanley Capital International Index, which reflects all major stock markets outside North America, gained 904%, more than threefold the 277% increase of the U.S. market.

Investing in international stocks is an excellent way to diversify a stock portfolio. In *A Random Walk Down Wall Street*, Burton Malkiel writes that over a 21-year period from 1977 to 1997, the mix of stocks that provided the highest return available with the least risk was 24% in the developed foreign country stocks (Europe, Australia, and Far East) and 76% in U.S. stocks.

An investment in a foreign stock can lead to a profit or loss in two ways:

1. The price of the stock in its local currency can advance or decline.

2. Relative to the U.S. dollar, the value of the foreign currency may rise or fall.

The optimal situation is to have the price of the stock rise in the local currency *and* the value of the foreign currency rise against the U.S. dollar. Of the several methods for investing in foreign stocks, the three most popular for individual investors are (1) American Depositary Receipts (2) mutual funds, and (3) Webs (see Key 34).

American Depositary Receipts (ADRs). Individuals who wish to purchase foreign securities should purchase ADRs, which are negotiable receipts representing ownership of stock in a foreign corporation traded on an exchange. ADRs are issued only on widely held and actively traded corporations. Further, they are very liquid and have transaction costs comparable to U.S. stocks. They are issued by a U.S. bank and represent shares on deposit with that bank's foreign office or custodian. ADRs allow investors to buy or sell foreign stocks without actually taking physical possession of the underlying securities. Purchase is made in U.S. dollars, and dividends are received in U.S. dollars.

By the end of 1998, 505 ADRs were listed on the NYSE, AMEX, and NASDAQ, up from a total of 176 in 1990. Counting private ADRs, which are not listed and are more difficult for an individual to trade, the total grew to 1,415 from 836 in 1990. The best Web site for information and prices is *www.adr.com.*

Mutual funds. The easiest way to invest in foreign securities is to purchase shares in a mutual fund that invests in such securities. This course of action would be preferable for investors who lack the time or inclination to investigate foreign markets. International stock funds offer the advantage of participation in a diversified portfolio of foreign stocks in addition to professional management. International funds are available that specialize in particular regions, such as Asia, or specific countries, such as Brazil or Germany. Prior to purchasing any of these funds, a copy of the prospectus should be obtained,

125

which describes the investment philosophy of the fund. Some international stock mutual funds that have been especially good performers are listed below:

- Tweedy, Brown Global Value (800-432-4789)
- Europacific Growth (800-421-4120)
- Schwab International Index (800-435-4000)
- Janus Worldwide (800-525-8983)
- Artisan International (800-344-1770)

41

CONVERTIBLE SECURITIES

A convertible security refers to a bond or a preferred stock that can be exchanged for common stock at a certain price or within a particular time frame. Once it has been exchanged or converted into common stock, the security cannot be converted back. Convertible bonds provide investors with a fixed interest payment. Convertible preferred stock provides investors with a stated dividend. Holders of these securities can reap the benefits of rising stock prices while insulated from the effects of falling prices. Aided by the rise of the stock market over the last five years, convertible bond funds were the best-performing category of bond fund—and they also were the best over the recent three years.

Convertible bonds. Convertible bonds generally have a face or par value of $1000 for each bond, meaning that the corporation promises to pay $1000 to the holder at maturity. In addition, the company also pays a fixed rate of interest, which typically is less than the interest on a nonconvertible bond because of the value of the conversion feature. Investors are willing to accept a lower rate of interest in return for the opportunity to participate in the appreciation of the common stock.

Convertible preferred stock. Convertible preferred stocks are not as prevalent as convertible bonds. Most convertible preferred stocks are issued as a result of mergers, to provide income to holders of the security without diluting the common stock of the acquiring company. The rights of preferred stockholders are subordinate to those of bondholders in distributions and in any corporate liquidation; however, dividends must be paid on preferred stock before any dividends can be paid on common stock. Similar to convertible bonds, convertible preferred stocks provide a fixed dividend while allowing participation in the appreciation of the price of the common stock through the right of conversion.

Advantages to the investor. Convertible securities combine the safety and fixed income of bonds or preferred stocks with the potential for capital appreciation of common stocks. Actually, holders of convertible securities do not even have to redeem their securities to participate in rising stock prices. Typically, the price of the convertible security will rise with the price of the stock, although it never rises as much. Alternatively, if the stock price declines, the price of the convertible also will decline, again by not as much. In the latter case, the interest specified on the convertible bond or the dividend on the convertible preferred stock serves to brake the decline in price.

Many of the companies issuing convertible securities are smaller companies with speculative common stock. Typically, many of these companies have a low dividend yield on their common stock, making the common stock an unattractive investment for those investors desiring current return. Convertible securities provide these individuals with an alternative way to invest in the possible growth of the company while earning a good current return.

As a general rule, convertible securities are *callable*, which means a company can redeem the security for cash. Seldom are they actually redeemed, however. The purpose of the call provision is to force conversion of the issue when the conversion value of the security is significantly above the call price. If the convertible security is called when the market value of the stock is greater than the conversion value of the bond, conversion is advisable.

Convertible securities are denoted by the initials "cv" in the current yield column of the bond tables. Surveys of convertible securities are published regularly in Standard & Poor's *Bond Guide*.

42

STOCK OPTIONS

Trading volume in stock options has grown remarkably since the creation of the Chicago Board Options Exchange (CBOE) in 1973. The listed option has become a practical investment vehicle for institutions and individuals seeking profit or protection. The CBOE is the world's largest options marketplace, with about half the share of the total options market. Options also are traded on the AMEX, the Pacific Stock Exchange, and the Philadelphia Stock Exchange. Options are written on common stock, securities, and other goods. The CBOE trades options on listed and over-the-counter stocks, Standard & Poor's 100 and 500 Indexes, Russell 2000 Index, NASDAQ-100 Index, DJIA, Internet Commerce Index, and others.

What are options? An option is a contract that provides to its holder (buyer) the right to purchase from or sell to the issuer (writer) a specified interest at a designated price called the exercise price (striking price) for a given period of time. Therefore, three conditions are specified in options contracts:

1. Property to be delivered
2. Price of the property
3. Specified time period during which the right held by the buyer can be exercised

Options have standardized terms, including the exercise price and the expiration time. This standardization makes it possible for buyers or writers of options to close out their positions by offsetting sales and purchases. By selling an option with the same terms as the one purchased, or buying an option with the same terms as the

129

one sold, an investor can liquidate a position at any time.

Two types of option contracts exist—the *call option* and the *put option*. A call option gives the buyer the right to purchase a specified quantity of the underlying interest at a fixed price at any time during the life of the option. For example, an option to buy 100 shares of the common stock of ABC Corporation is an "ABC call option."

Alternatively, a put option gives the buyer the right to sell a specified quantity of the underlying interest at a fixed price at any time during the life of the option. An option to sell 100 shares of common stock of ABC Corporation at a particular price is an "ABC put option."

Options nomenclature. Certain terminology is unique to options trading. Some of the more important terms follow:

- *Option writer.* The seller or issuer of an option contract. For example, if the buyer of the option exercises an ABC call option, the option writer is obligated to deliver the required number of shares of ABC common stock.
- *Option buyer or holder.* The buyer of an option contract. For example, the buyer of an ABC call or put option has the right, although not the obligation, to purchase or sell, respectively, shares of ABC Corporation common stock at a specified price within a specified period of time.
- *Exercise or striking price.* The price at which the holder can sell to or buy from the writer the item underlying the option. For example, an ABC 50 call option gives the buyer the right to purchase 100 shares of ABC stock at a price of $50 per share. On the other hand, an ABC 40 put option gives the buyer the right to sell 100 shares of ABC Corporation common stock at a price of $40 per share.
- *Expiration date.* The last date on which the buyer is entitled to exercise an option. However, if an option is not exercised or sold prior to that expiration

date, it is worthless.

- *Premium.* The price that the buyer of an option pays (and that the writer of an option receives) for the option. Premiums vary in response to such variables as the relationship between the exercise price and the current market value of the underlying security, the volatility of the underlying security, the amount of time remaining until the expiration date, current interest rates, and the effect of supply and demand in the options market.
- *Out-of-the-money option.* When the striking price of a call option is higher than the market price of the underlying interest, or when the striking price of the put option is lower than the market value of the underlying interest, it is "out of the money."
- *In-the-money option.* When the striking price of a call option is lower than the market value of the underlying interest, or when the striking price of a put option is higher than the market price of the underlying interest, it is "in the money."

Options versus stock. Options traded on exchanges, such as the CBOE, are similar in many respects to securities traded on other exchanges:

- Options are listed securities.
- Orders to buy or sell options are handled by brokers in the same manner as orders to buy and sell stock. Similarly, orders on listed options are executed on the trading floor of a national exchange where trading is conducted in an auction market.
- The price, volume, and other information about options are almost instantly available, as is the case with stocks.

Differences between stocks and options are as follows:

- Unlike shares of common stock, there is no fixed number of options. The number of options depends upon the number of buyers and sellers.

- Unlike stocks, there are no certificates as evidence of ownership. Printed statements prepared by the individual brokerage firms indicate ownership of options.
- An option is a wasting asset. If an option is not sold or exercised prior to the expiration date, it becomes worthless. The holder therefore loses the full purchase price.

Who should buy options? Options have some definite advantages. First, the maximum loss is limited to the premium paid for the option. Maximum loss exposure is determinable in advance in the event the optioned security moves against expectations. In addition, options can produce quick profits with little capital investment. Finally, options are flexible and can be combined with other investments to protect positions and make profits.

However, only those investors with well-defined investment objectives and a plan for realizing those objectives should trade in options. Successful options traders thoroughly research options, understand options strategies, and closely follow the options market on a day-to-day basis. Explanatory material on options trading is available from the CBOE Web site (*www.cboe.com*).

43

FINANCIAL FUTURES

A futures contract is an agreement between seller and buyer, respectively, to deliver and take delivery of a commodity or security at a specified future date. Financial futures are contracts written on securities, currency, or various stock indexes. Unlike commodity futures, delivery does not involve a physical commodity. Rather, financial securities or cash are involved in any delivery needed to fulfill the contract.

Borrowers, lenders, investors, and others protect their investments by hedging with financial futures. Institutions and individuals can take positions in the futures market to protect the gains they have made in the cash market. Speculators also can use futures to profit from anticipated changes in interest rates, foreign exchange rates, or movements in the stock market. However, caution is necessary. This market is extremely speculative, and only a small percentage of an investment portfolio should be committed to trading financial futures. As a general rule, small investors should avoid the futures markets to avoid losing money.

Development of the financial futures market. Commodities futures trading began in the United States in the mid-19th century, originally to smooth out the seasonal supply and demand of agricultural products. Since that time, these futures have grown into a huge market for speculation and hedging by many different participants. Futures for precious metals, foreign currencies, and other monetary vehicles have since evolved.

The futures market for U.S. Treasury bonds, introduced in 1977, represented the initial market in financial futures. The wide acceptance and use of these instruments led to the introduction of futures representing a wide variety of financial instruments. For example, futures trading includes Treasury bills, bonds, and notes, Ginnie Maes, 90-day certificates of deposit, 90-day Eurodollars, and several stock indexes.

Financial futures are traded on a regulated exchange complete with established rules for the performance of contracts. The exchange clearinghouse acts as a third party and guarantor to all transactions, thus eliminating the need for sellers and buyers to become known to one another. While a future is a commitment to buy or sell at some point in the future, delivery of the underlying instrument rarely occurs. Trades in futures contracts are settled by entering into the offsetting position. By 1999, more than 65% of all futures trades in the United States were financial futures. Based upon these figures, financial futures appear to be fulfilling an important need.

Arithmetic of financial futures trading. Perhaps more than any other form of speculation or investment, gains and losses in futures trading are highly leveraged. In fact, only a small amount of cash (called *margin*) is required to buy or sell a futures contract. The smaller the margin in comparison to the value of the futures contract, the greater the leverage. For example, assume that in anticipation of rising stock prices, an investor buys one June S&P 500 stock index futures contract at a time when the June index is trading at 1,300. Also, assume the initial margin requirement is $23,000. Because the value of the futures contract is $250 times the index, each one-point change in the index represents a $250 gain or loss.

An increase in the index from 1,300 to 1,392 would double the $23,000 margin deposit, and a decrease from 1,300 to 1,208 would eliminate the margin. All it takes is a 7% change in the stock index to produce a 100% gain or loss. Low margin requirements sharply increase the profit or loss potential. A clear understanding of the concept of leverage (see Key 28) as well as the amount of gain or loss that will result from any given change in the futures price of the particular futures contract traded is essential for anyone who ventures into this market.

Further information on futures can be obtained from the Chicago Board of Trade's Web site (*www.cbot.com*) or the Chicago Mercantile Exchange's Web site (*www.cme.com*).

44

RISK AND DIVERSIFICATION

As shown in the first Key, common stocks have, on average, proven to be excellent investments. With an average return of about 11%, common stocks have outperformed corporate bonds and government securities. However, investors should take into account the risks associated with these generous returns. In 1973–74, the Dow Jones Industrial Average (DJIA) dropped almost by half, from 1,051.70 to 577.60. On October 19, 1987 the stock market collapsed, free-falling 508 points. This drop was 22.6%, even greater than the storied crash of October 29, 1929, when the DJIA lost 12.8% of its value. The stock market never has climbed upward in a smooth, predictable pattern. Periodically, there have been steep losses, jarring the confidence of jittery investors. There have been nine bear markets during the period 1945–1999—defined as a drop of more than 20% in the DJIA. The last one occurred in 1990 with a drop of 21.2% in the 87-day period ending on October 11, 1990. Stockholders should not panic when these drops occur, rather they should be viewed as potential opportunities.

Any investment involves a tradeoff between risk and reward. The higher the reward an investor seeks, the greater the risks and uncertainties are likely to be. Stock pickers who beat the market in one period or another may have assumed great risk. Wise investors examine a strategy's level of risk in addition to its performance.

Although common stock certainly has proved to be rewarding for investors, there are risks and uncertainties, as discussed throughout this book. Investments in common stocks will fluctuate in price over a substantial range, especially if held for several years. Do not expect to buy a stock at its low price for the year. Individual investors should be looking at a time horizon of three to five years. Ultimately, it will be the company's success in generating future earnings that will most influence the price of its stock. However, over any given period, stock prices will fluctuate widely in response to company news, changes in industry conditions, the overall economic and political climate, unexpected events, and shifts in investor psychology.

Diversification. One proven method to reduce risk is for investors to diversify their holdings. This strategy does not mean that an investor must acquire 50 different stocks. Diversification depends not only on the number of stocks an investor owns, but also on the types of stocks chosen. Investment risks are related to different economic variables, including consumer spending, business investment, and interest rates. If an investor has ten stocks, all in the utility industry, the portfolio is not diversified. These stocks likely will move together in response to changes in interest rates, for example. Even a portfolio of stocks in the airline, auto, and steel industries tends to be cyclical, so the stocks will be strongly influenced by changes in the business cycle. Investors should select stocks that do not follow the same pattern in response to changes in economic variables.

How many stocks comprise a relatively diversified portfolio? Martin Zweig, in *Winning on Wall Street*, says that investors with between $5,000 and $20,000 should buy four or five stocks. A $50,000 portfolio should include eight or nine stocks. At $100,000, a dozen stocks is appropriate. Finally, at $250,000, he recommends a portfolio of roughly 20 stocks. Beyond that, for greater amounts of capital, he believes that 33 stocks offer sufficient diversification.

45

DOLLAR COST
AVERAGING

Peter Lynch, former portfolio manager of Fidelity Magellan, says that predicting the short-term direction of the market is futile. In his book *One Up on Wall Street*, he says that investors should concentrate on picking stocks and not attempt to predict the market as a whole. Over the long haul, it can be costly not to invest in stocks. The approximate 11% average yearly return since 1926 indicates how profitable stock investments are in the long run. Data for the Standard & Poor's 500 Stock Index since 1926 indicate that the odds of losing money in stocks over one year are around 30%. However, over ten years, the risk of loss falls to just 3%.

Given the difficulty in predicting market turns, what strategy should an investor follow? One of the oldest and best of all formula plans is what is known as *dollar cost averaging*, or the constant dollar plan. Dollar cost averaging requires that an investor commit a fixed amount of funds to stocks at specific time intervals—monthly, quarterly, or whatever period is most suitable to the investor's saving schedule. The technique is very mechanical at one level, requiring no forecast of the direction of the market. It is not a trading system, but rather a long-term investment program.

Under this program, the average cost of stocks in a portfolio should be less than the average market price of the stocks. This phenomenon occurs because a constant amount of dollars purchases fewer shares at higher prices and more shares at lower prices. Consider the following example:

Example. Suppose $500 is invested every three months over the next year. Assume the price of the stock or mutual fund is $20 the first quarter, $10 the second, $20 the third, and $10 in the last quarter. In the first quarter, 25 shares at $20 each were acquired for a total of $500. In the second quarter, $500 bought 50 shares. Then, at the end of the four quarters, 150 shares will have been acquired with the $2,000 investment, at an average cost of $13.33 per share. However, during the year, the average price of the shares was $15.

Although dollar cost averaging produces the best results with stocks that fluctuate substantially, the average investor should avoid stocks that are too volatile. The best policy is to buy high-quality stocks that will continue to produce above-average growth in revenue and earnings. Obviously, money cannot be made on a stock when its price continually moves downward.

The key to dollar cost averaging is to find the patience to continue the contributions through good and bad market periods. To begin with, $250 to $500 per month is a good investment strategy. The low cost of using mutual funds makes them good candidates for starting a program. Many of them feature automatic investment plans whereby an amount of money specified by the investor is electronically transferred from a bank account and invested in a mutual fund on a regular basis.

46

401(K) RETIREMENT PLANS

Named after the applicable section of the federal law, the 401(K) plan is an outstanding way to build a retirement nest egg. Most large companies sponsor 401(K) plans or similar tax-deferred retirement plans, and many smaller companies have adopted them as well. The plan provides employees with an automatic way to save for retirement while reducing and deferring taxes. Everyone should take advantage of this benefit whenever it is available.

A 401(K) plan is a retirement plan that permits employees to defer paying taxes on a part of their salary. This contribution is deducted from the salary and is not counted as part of earnings for current income tax purposes. The maximum tax-free deduuction is adjusted each year for inflation. In 1999, the maximum deduction was $10,000. Taxpayers in the 28% bracket who made the maximum contribution of $10,000 in 1999 saved $2800 in federal income taxes.

What makes 401(K) plans even more enticing is that many companies match all or part of the employee contributions. They often, however, retain the option of claiming a portion of their matching contributions if the employee leaves the company before completing seven years of service. The company chooses the investment options. The typical choices have included the employer's stock, a stock mutual fund, a fund combining stocks and bonds, and so-called guaranteed investment contracts (GICs), which are insurance contracts that pay a fixed rate of interest, usually comparable to certificates of deposit.

However, we have moved from three or four options into an era where we see eight or even twelve options as commonplace. Guidelines on 401(K) retirement plans call for a broad range of investment alternatives in various risk categories and continuing education for employees about how these investments work. Although the provisions are not mandatory, employers generally are observing them, largely because following the guidelines assures some legal protection against liability in the event an investor loses money in a plan or makes poor choices.

Most people opt for the GIC option because they believe that these are the safest investments. That could be a big mistake. Locking in a guaranteed rate is not worth giving up the potential price gains in common stock. Although GIC contracts now return about 7% annually, this return is considerably less than the 11% that stocks historically have returned. Do not assume a 4% difference in return is insignificant. An investment of $10,000 with a return of 7% will grow to $54,270 when compounded over 25 years. In contrast, the same $10,000 when compounded at 11% over 25 years will grow to $133,855! Another mistake many employees make is to invest too much of their retirement plan money in their own company's stock. It is too risky to have a retirement nest egg dependent upon a single stock.

Almost everyone agrees that investors who are saving for retirement should put money in stocks. The question is, how much? The mutual fund company T. Rowe Price recommends 80% for someone 25 years from retirement. This allocation should gradually be reduced as a person ages. As retirement nears, some money should be shifted out of the volatile stock category. For someone five years away from retirement, T. Rowe Price suggests a stock allocation of 40%.

If a plan has an international stock option, up to 20 to 25% of the stock allocation may be devoted to it. Although the U.S. stock market has flourished in the

1990s, the international markets outperformed it in the 1970s and 1980s. Many of these will continue to grow faster than our own economy. An exposure to international markets offers the possibility of increasing return while reducing risk.

Participants can begin making 401(K) withdrawals without penalty after age 59½ or upon retirement or if they are permanently disabled. In all cases, participants must begin withdrawing 401(K) money by age 70½. The money can be withdrawn in a lump sum, but many plans also provide for the purchase of an annuity or installment payment. The withdrawals are subject to ordinary income tax.

Funds can be withdrawn before age 59½ without penalty only if an individual is facing a financial hardship. To be eligible for early withdrawals, proof that other financial resources have been exhausted is required before applying, and only the amount needed may be borrowed. If financial hardship cannot be proved, there is a 10% penalty for withdrawing funds prior to age 59½, in addition to paying income tax.

Many plans permit borrowing. Loans can be made for any reason the employer allows, and are not recognized as withdrawals because the money is scheduled to be paid back. Before borrowing against the plan, however, borrowers should ask what the interest rate on loans is and the term of repayment. Remember that dipping into 401(K) funds to pay short-term expenses can put a retirement nest egg at risk.

One of the most basic investment mistakes many employees make is not joining 401(K) plans. About 15 to 20% of eligible employees are not participating. The younger employees especially are apt to ignore these plans. They are making a serious error. The 401(K) plan is positively the best investment vehicle for an employee. It produces automatic savings, tax-deferred earnings, and "free" money from the employer. A 401(K) plan will be the chief source of retirement income for many retirees in the future.

However small the contribution, everyone eligible should contribute to a 401(K) plan. Those employees who can afford to contribute the maximum should definitely do so. Take full advantage of this saving option before investing elsewhere.

47

INVESTMENT CLUBS

One way for small investors to familiarize themselves with the stock market at little cost is to join an investment club. Investment clubs are groups of 10 to 20 individuals who get together to learn investment principles, build an investment portfolio, and exchange information. Most of these groups join together once a month, deposit their monthly investment—typically $50 to $75—review studies of stocks presented by members, and select a stock in which to invest. The liquidating values of shares are computed regularly. One member typically is designated as an agent for the group. Any member who wants to withdraw from the club will receive the liquidating value of his or her shares.

National Association of Investment Clubs. Many of the clubs belong to the National Association of Investment Clubs (NAIC), a nonprofit organization with annual dues of $40 per club plus $14 for each club member. For this price, they provide a manual that provides complete instructions for organizing and operating an investment club and offers assistance in the evaluation of stocks. In addition, there is a monthly magazine that comes with membership, *Better Investing*, which is an excellent investment education publication.

The NAIC has three classes of membership: individual, investment club, and corporate. Currently there are about 60,000 individual members, 250 corporate members, and 38,500 investment clubs consisting of about 730,000 members. The average club is five years old and has a portfolio worth about $40,500.

The NAIC lists four principles that provide a foundation for sound investing practice:

1. Invest a set sum once a month in common stocks, regardless of general market conditions. Doing so helps investors obtain lower average costs.
2. Reinvest dividends and capital gains immediately. Money grows faster if earnings are reinvested.
3. Buy growth stocks, which represent companies with sales and earnings that are increasing at an above-average rate.
4. Invest in different fields. Diversification helps spread both risk and opportunity.

Information about the NAIC can be obtained from 711 West Thirteen Mile Road, Madison Heights, Michigan 48071, 877-275-6242, or *www.better-investing.org*.

American Association of Individual Investors. The American Association of Individual Investors (AAII) is an "independent, nonprofit corporation formed for the purpose of assisting individuals in becoming effective managers of their own assets through programs of education, information, and research." This estimable organization, composed of 170,000 members, is an invaluable source of information to all investors, regardless of their expertise. The $49 annual membership fee includes a subscription to the monthly *AAII Journal* and the annual *The Individual Investor's Guide to Low-Load Mutual Funds.*

The monthly magazine provides articles that are written by prominent practitioners and academicians in different areas that reflect the latest thinking in the field. The annual guide to low-load funds is a comprehensive, easy-to-read comparison of more than 900 mutual funds. The data provided include a wide variety of risk and performance statistics of interest to investors.

In addition, the AAII has an investment home study program designed for those who want to enhance their understanding of investing. Concepts, strategies, and analytical methods for successful investing and portfolio management are explored in ten lessons. The program costs $55 for members, which includes free updates and revisions. Information about the AAII can be obtained from its office at 625 North Michigan Avenue, Suite 1900, Chicago, Illinois 60611 (800-428-2244) or *www.aaii.com.*

48

INVESTMENT SCAMS

Every year, the financial media reports on an investment scam that has duped unwary investors. Investors continue to put their money in scams that clearly ought to arouse suspicion. In 1999, affinity groups fraud became a serious concern. This type of fraud is perpetrated on religious, ethnic, and professional groups by members of these groups or persons enjoying the trust of these groups.

Ponzi schemes. A 30-year-old immigrant, Charles Ponzi, etched his name in the annals of history in 1920 when he made an offer that thousands of investors could not refuse—a 50% return in just six weeks. By the time the scheme began to unravel six months later, Ponzi had pocketed $10 million. His name has become synonymous with confidence games in which some early investors earn excellent returns, paid off with funds obtained from later participants in the scheme, who lose everything. Variations on the Ponzi scheme have duped investors over and over again. When the demand for new participants exhausts the supply, the Ponzi pyramid collapses, crushing the hopes of its "investors." The lesson here is to be skeptical about a guarantee of far higher interest rates or returns than that prevailing in the marketplace.

Stock scams. Any investment that guarantees an unusually high rate of return should be regarded as suspect. The penny stock market, which consists of stocks selling for less than $1 per share, has been a continuing source of headaches to securities regulators. Investors are bilked by swindlers who prey on those who substitute greed for sound judgment. The emergence of computerized dialing and cheap long-distance phone rates has allowed smooth-talking brokers working out of "boiler rooms" to contact millions of people. They offer stock in small companies for a few cents per share, promising huge profits in a short time. Investors should be wary of the penny stock market.

Internet fraud. Both the SEC and North American Securities Administrators Association (NASAA) have identified Internet fraud as a major area of concern. The SEC now gets as many as 300 E-mails per day from investors reporting potential Internet frauds, up from just a dozen three years ago. The NASAA has uncovered a wide variety of scams using the schemes, insider trading, and acting as a broker or investment adviser without proper licensure.

Phony financial planners. A growing number of crooks are exploiting individuals concerned about their financial well-being by- selling them bogus investments and worthless counseling. Most of this fraud is perpetrated not by financial planners, but by individuals posing as financial planners. Investors can reduce their chances of falling prey to a charlatan by checking the backgrounds of financial planners and other professionals with the National Association of Securities Dealers' Public Disclosure Web site (*www.nasdr.com/2000.htm*). Requests for information generally can be processed in five to ten days. The cost for businesses is $30; the service is free to individuals.

If an individual wishes to avoid dubious investments and scams, *StockDetective.com* alerts users to Wall Street "No Gooders," who are targets of SEC actions. It also presents "Stinky Stocks," targeting companies with stocks of questionable value.

49

INVESTMENT STRATEGIES

Are there certain stratagems that investors can follow to generate stock market gains? Yes, there are. However, investors should remember not to follow any strategy blindly. Ultimately, the important point is the factors that drive these strategies. Investors should understand the nature of the stocks they own and the specific reasons for holding the stocks.

Low P/E ratios. Academic research has found that low P/E stocks consistently produce larger long-term returns than high P/E stocks. David Dreman, in *The Contrarian Investment Strategy*, makes observations about this relationship. He states that, in the aggregate, companies for which the strongest growth is projected do not meet market expectations of earnings growth, and companies with supposedly the worst prospects often do not do as poorly as investors anticipate. Investors who follow this strategy need to observe the following guidelines:

- Determine that the company's financial condition is strong. A low P/E ratio might be justified by the market's concern about the risk associated with a company's large debt position.
- Look for solid earnings growth (at least 15% per year over the last five years).
- Be cautious about cyclical companies. A low P/E ratio may reflect the fact that earnings are at a cyclical peak.

Look for smaller companies. Stocks with market capitalization (price multiplied by the number of shares outstanding) between $100 million and $500 million have outperformed larger stocks after adjusting for risk. The earnings of smaller companies can grow faster than those of larger companies, because they are starting from a far smaller base. A more aggressive investor might want to include a few emerging growth companies in his or her portfolio (see Key 38). Some guidelines to follow:

- Look for earnings growth of 20% to 25% over the last five years.
- Determine if the company can maintain or increase this growth rate.
- Make certain that its debt load is reasonable. Small companies with large debt can get into serious financial difficulties if an economic downturn occurs.

Low institutional ownership. Common stocks that are widely held by institutions tend to not do as well as stocks with little or no institutional ownership. The best time to buy a stock is *before* the institutions become attracted to it and run up the price.

Insider buying. Companies that report a high level of insiders' purchases perform better than companies reporting heavy sales by insiders (defined as officers, directors, or a stockholder who owns more than 5% of the stock). The SEC requires the disclosure of this information, which is reported by *Barron's, Investor's Business Daily, The Wall Street Journal,* and various Web sites (e.g., *www.quote.yahoo.com*).

Avoid penny stocks. This market is fraught with stock manipulation and fraud. Buying these stocks is more akin to gambling than investing (see Key 48).

50

RETIREMENT PLANNING

This Key is not intended to be a comprehensive guide to retirement planning. Its purpose is to emphasize the role of common stocks in any plan that is established. In addition, Web sites that are helpful for retirement planning are provided here. A recent survey of Americans discovered that nearly one third are not saving for retirement and a large percentage of the rest are saving insufficient amounts. Only 20% to 25% is confident that they will have saved enough to comfortably retire.

The strategy adopted to plan for retirement is critical. First, there are some fundamental determinants of the amount that will be available upon retirement. There are three factors that will determine the amount accumulated at retirement:

1. Amount of money invested
2. The percent return on that investment
3. The period of time the investment accumulates

Compounding. The English economist John Maynard Keynes referred to compound interest as "magic." Compound interest is interest on interest that compounds when it remains in the account, becoming part of the principal that earns further interest. It is important to remember that compounding works only if interest or dividends are reinvested. The magic in compounding is the tremendous rate at which savings can mount over the years. If $2,000 per year is invested starting at the age of 30, with a return of 10% each year, a total of $542,049 will have accumulated at age 65. Therefore, a $70,000

151

investment ($2,000 per year for 35 years) has accumulated to $542,049.

Another example of the magic of compounding illustrates the importance of starting early in a savings plan. Suppose $2,000 per year is invested for 10 years from the age of 25 and then nothing is saved for the next 30 years. Assuming a 10% yearly return, the amount that would accumulate at age 65 would be $556,197. A $20,000 cash outlay ($2,000 per year for 10 years) has grown to $556,197.

An alternative strategy would be to save nothing until age 35 and then save $2,000 per year until age 65. That cash outlay of $60,000 ($2,000 per year for 30 years) would grow to $328,588—an impressive sum but considerably less than the $556,197 that the previous strategy would produce. The lesson: save early, save regularly, and let compounding do the rest!

Role of common stocks. Despite the evidence of the period from 1982 to 1998 (the stock market only declined in 1990), corrections (usually considered a 10% decline from peak to trough) occur fairly frequently. In this century, the market has declined 10% about every 1.5 years.

But what is amazing is the long-run consistency of the returns from holding common stocks. Jeremy Siegel has determined the returns from holding common stocks from the period 1802 to 1997 in his book *Stocks for the Long Run* (highly recommended). During those 195 years, the average after-inflation rate of returns for stocks was 7.0% between 1802 and 1870, 6.6% between 1871 and 1925, and 7.2% between 1926 and 1997. These gains trounced those of bonds and gold over the same period, and Siegel's book also demonstrates that, in the long run, stocks have been much safer than bonds.

The evidence is convincing that stocks should constitute the overwhelming proportion of all long-term financial portfolios. What percentage should stocks be in a portfolio? There is an old rule of thumb that stocks, as a percentage of a portfolio, should equal 100 minus the investor's age. That standard is okay, but a portfolio allocation should be based on risk tolerance and time horizon, and not only on age. Even 65-year-olds need to plan for inflation 15 to 20 years into their future.

A better rule would be to divide goals into short term (less than 3 years), intermediate (3 to 10 years), and long term (more than 10 years). Money needed in three years can be put in money market funds or Certificates of Deposit (CDs). For intermediate goals, 75% stocks and 25% income investments would be a good mix. If planning for beyond ten years, a diversified portfolio of common stocks makes sense. Those investors not comfortable doing their own stock picking should buy highly diversified mutual funds with low expense ratios. Index funds, in particular, have these characteristics.

Information. Retirement planning information is increasingly available on the Internet. Several excellent Web sites will help individuals figure out if—and when—they can afford to retire. They offer interactive worksheets that request age, assets, and other numbers, and will offer advice about asset allocation. Both *SmartMoney* (*www.smartmoney.com/ac/retirement*) and *Money* (*www.moneymag.com*) offer this service. T. Rowe Price (*www.troweprice.com*) and Vanguard (*www.vanguard.com*) also offer excellent planning guides. Finally, the American Savings Education Council *(www.asec.org)* provides a useful retirement planning calculator.

We highly recommend *A Random Walk Down Wall Street* by Burton Malkiel as a classic book on investing in general and retirement planning in particular. The chapter "A Life-Cycle Guide to Investing" is an outstanding contribution to this subject.

QUESTIONS AND ANSWERS

What is the difference between a primary market and a secondary market for common stocks?

The sale of new securities, including stocks, to raise funds is a primary market transaction. The proceeds of the sale of these securities represent new capital for the issuing company. New issues typically are underwritten by investment bankers who acquire the total issue from the company. They then resell these securities in smaller units to individual and institutional investors.

After a new issue of securities is sold in the primary market, subsequent trades of the security take place in the secondary market. The secondary market is vital because it provides liquidity to investors who acquire securities in the primary market.

What is the major reason for the existence of regional stock exchanges? How do they differ from the national stock exchanges?

Regional stock exchanges trade the securities of local companies that are not large enough to qualify for listing on one of the national exchanges. As a result, the listing requirements are not as stringent as those of the New York Stock Exchange (NYSE) or the American Stock Exchange (AMEX). In addition, regional exchanges list companies also listed on a national exchange for brokers who are not members of a national exchange. This dual listing permits local brokerage firms, which are not members of the NYSE, to trade shares of dual-listed stock using their regional exchange membership. Membership on a regional exchange typically is much less expensive than a national exchange.

What is the relationship between NASDAQ and the over-the-counter (OTC) market?

The OTC market is the largest segment of the secondary market in terms of the number of securities (nearly 13,000). Although OTC stocks represent many small and unseasoned companies, the range of securities traded is very wide. This market is a negotiated market in which investors directly negotiate purchases and sales through dealers.

The NASDAQ system is computerized, providing current bid and ask prices on more than 6,000 of the most widely traded OTC securities. Through a dealer, a broker instantly can discover the bid and ask quotations offered by all dealers making a market in a stock. The broker can then contact the dealer offering the best price and negotiate a trade directly.

Are there any drawbacks to following the Dow Jones Industrial Average (DJIA) as a measure of market performance? Are there other stock market indicators?

The DJIA is the most widely followed barometer of stock price movements. However, the index consists of only 30 large "blue-chip" companies. In addition, the DJIA is price weighted, meaning that the component stock prices are added together and the result is divided by another figure called the divisor. As a result, a high-priced stock has a greater influence on the index than a low-priced stock. A significant fluctuation in the price of one or several of the stocks in the index can distort the average.

After the DJIA, Standard & Poor's (S&P) 500 Stock Index is the most widely followed stock index. On a daily basis, its movement is more representative of the movement of the stock market as a whole than the DJIA because of its larger size (500 stocks) and the fact that the index is market weighted. In a market-weighted average, both the price and number of shares outstanding enter into the computation.

Why should an investor hold a diversified portfolio? What is the simplest way to diversify?

Diversification can reduce the risk associated with investments to a substantial degree. Diversification can be thought of as "not putting all of your eggs into one basket." An effectively diversified portfolio reduces risk without cutting long-run average return. In selecting stocks, investors should be careful to select stocks with risks related to different economic, political, and social factors.

A diversified portfolio is very difficult to achieve when investable funds are limited. For those investors in this position, a mutual fund offers the opportunity to participate in an investment pool that can contain hundreds of different securities.

What is a growth stock?

A growth stock is defined as stock of a company with earnings that have significantly outstripped the earnings of other companies in the past and are expected to do so in the future. These companies tend to reinvest a large part of their earnings and thus pay a relatively low (or no) dividend to stockholders. Investors who purchase these shares are more concerned with the appreciation in the market price of the stock than they are with the receipt of cash dividends.

Because these stocks provide little current income, they are dependent upon high growth rates to sustain a high stock price. If these growth rates do not materialize, the stock price can fall dramatically. As a consequence, investors in growth stocks should be aware of the greater risks associated with the possibility of earning superior returns.

What is the difference between a *bull market* and a *bear market*? What are the implications of each to the investor?

A bull market is a prolonged rise in the price of stocks; a bear market is a prolonged decline in the price of stocks. Stock market movements are extremely important to investors. Historical studies indicate that 60% of stock price movements are directly related to movements in the overall market; 30% to 35% are related to sector or group movements; and only 5% are related to individual stock movements.

Because stock prices generally have risen over time, bull markets predominate over bear markets. In fact, the market typically rises two out of every three years. Although bear markets tend to be of substantially shorter duration than bull markets, the decline can be steep. Excluding the crash of 1929–1932, when stock prices plunged 89%, the average bear market is about 30% from peak to trough.

How does a stock warrant differ from a call option? Which is riskier?

Warrants are options to acquire a fixed number of common shares at a predetermined price during a specified time period. The definition is similar to a call option with some essential differences. First, warrants are issued by the company that issued the stock rather than by an independent option writer. Second, the life of a warrant usually is much longer than the life of a call option; the typical term for warrants may vary from two years to perpetuity.

For investors, warrants are pure speculation. Leverage works both ways. Warrant prices go up or down faster than the underlying stock. In this sense, they are similar to options. Their advantage over options is that the longer period to expiration gives the investor the opportunity to speculate on a company over a longer term.

What is the difference between open-end and closed-end funds?

Two basic types of funds exist: (1) closed-end funds and (2) open-end funds. A closed-end fund is an investment company with a fixed number of shares that trade on an exchange or over-the-counter. Similar to common stocks, the price of these funds changes as demand for the shares changes. Many of these funds trade at a discount from their net asset value (assets less liabilities). Information on closed-end funds is available at the Web site run by the Closed-End Fund Association (*www.closed-endfunds.com*).

Open-end funds, by far the most popular type of fund, issue or redeem shares at the net asset value of the portfolio. Unlike closed-end funds, the number of shares is not fixed, but instead increases as investors purchase more shares. These shares are not traded on any market and always are worth the following value: assets minus liabilities divided by the number of shares.

What are some fees associated with mutual fund investments?

Until recently, mutual funds were either load or no-load. Fee structures now are more complex and often are not made clear to investors. Among these fees are redemption fees, also called contingent deferred sales charges or back-end loads. A redemption fee is charged if an investor sells his or her shares, usually within a fixed period. It may be a flat percentage of the sales price or may be based on a sliding scale, say 5% the first year, declining in steps to 0% in the fifth year from the date of investment.

Under the controversial 12b-1 plans, the fund can charge a fee to pay for its marketing and promotion costs. A 12b-1 fee can be levied on the full value of the investment each year or on the original value of the investment.

All funds also charge a management fee to compensate the asset managers for their services. These fees range from around 2.0% of the fund assets to 2.5%.

Information on fees and other expense data is available on page 2 of every mutual fund prospectus. Investors should always read this page before purchasing shares in a mutual fund. Investors do not always get what they pay for. Thus, the funds that charge the highest fees do not necessarily increase in value faster than the "cheaper" funds.

How does the Securities and Exchange Commission (SEC) serve investors?

The SEC was established by Congress in 1934 to administer federal laws that seek to provide protection for investors. The overriding purpose of these laws is to ensure the integrity of the financial markets by requiring full and fair disclosure of material facts about companies offering securities for sale to the public.

The SEC does not insure investments. Nor does it prevent the sale of securities by risky, poorly managed, or unprofitable companies. Rather, registration with the SEC is designed to provide adequate and honest disclosures about a company and the securities it plans to sell. A portion of the information included in the required registration statement is included in a prospectus that is readily available to investors.

The SEC requires ongoing disclosure of a company's activities following the initial registration. Ongoing disclosure consists of annual, quarterly, and special reports. Form 10-K, the annual report, contains a myriad of financial data and nonfinancial information, including the names of corporate officers and directors and the extent of their ownership. Form 10-Q, the quarterly report, contains condensed financial and nonfinancial interest. Form 8-K, the report of significant events, reports changes of interest to the investing public (e.g., change of executive officer, change of audit firm). All of these forms can be obtained from the company or the SEC.

Does a balance sheet disclose the current market value of a company's assets?

Generally, the answer is *no*. Items reflected under property, plant, and equipment on the asset side of the balance sheet are reported at original cost less accumulated depreciation. The current market value of these assets is not reflected in the balance sheet or elsewhere in the financial statements. For many corporations, the amount shown for property, plant, and equipment is but a small percentage of the current market value of those assets.

The balance sheet also fails to disclose certain assets of vital importance to the company. For example, the value of a company's human resources or intellectual capacity is not reflected in the balance sheet. Additionally, the value of brand names often is not disclosed. If it is disclosed, the value refers to "unamortized cost" and has no relationship to current market value. In recent years, the purpose of many takeovers has been to acquire valuable brand names.

GLOSSARY

Arbitrage profiting from differences in price when the same security is traded on two or more markets.

Balance sheet financial statement showing a company's assets, liabilities, and owners' equity as of a specific date in time.

Bear person who believes that stock prices will drop.

Bear market prolonged period of declining prices. These periods usually last at least several months, and sometimes a year or more.

Big Board traders' term for the New York Stock Exchange (NYSE).

Bull person who believes that stock prices will rise.

Bull market prolonged increase in the prices of securities. These markets usually last at least several months, sometimes several years.

Callable the option of a company to "call" in a security and redeem it for cash.

Call option right of a buyer to purchase a specified quantity of a security interest at a fixed price at any time during the life of the option.

Common stock fractional shares of ownership in a corporation.

Convertible security bond or preferred stock that can be exchanged into a specified number of common shares at a specified price.

Diamonds index products that trade on the AMEX and track the Dow Jones Industrial Average.

Discount rate rate of interest charged by the Federal Reserve (Fed) to member banks.

Diversification an attempt to reduce the overall risk of a portfolio by owning different securities, rather than concentrating all of one's money in one or two stocks.

Dividend reimbursement plan automatic reinvestment of stockholder dividends in more shares of the company's stock.

Dividends payments representing a distribution of earnings made by a corporation to its stockholders.

Earnings per share amount of net income attributable to each share of common stock.

Federal Reserve Board consists of seven members who oversee the formulation of monetary policy and control of the money supply. Known as the Fed.

Financial leverage accelerative effect of debt on financial returns.

Financial ratios indicators of a company's financial performance and position.

401(K) plan investment that allows an employee to contribute pretax dollars up to a stated limit to a company pool, which is invested with the capital and earnings compounding on a tax-deferred basis until the employee retires or otherwise discontinues service.

Fundamental analysis process of estimating a security's value by analyzing the basic financial and economic facts about the company that issues the security.

Golden parachute lucrative compensation guaranteed to top executives in the event of a takeover.

Greenmail purchase by a corporation of its own stock from a potential acquirer at a price substantially greater than the market price. In exchange, the acquirer agrees to drop the takeover bid.

Hedging actions taken by investors to reduce a possible loss.

Income statement financial statement showing a company's revenues and expenses over a period of time.

Initial Public Offering (IPO) corporation's first offering of its own stock to the public.

Investment banking industry that specializes in assisting corporations and governments in marketing new securities.

Junk bond a high-risk, high-yield bond (less than BBB rating), generally issued either by a new company or to fund a corporate takeover.

Leveraged buyout process of buying a corporation's stock with borrowed money, then repaying at least part of the debt from the corporation's assets.

Liquidity the ease with which an asset can be converted into cash, reflecting a company's ability to meet its short-term obligations.

Load fund type of mutual fund where the buyer must pay a sales fee, or commission, on top of the price.

Margin trading using borrowed funds for trading; trading on credit, as governed by Federal Reserve and stock exchange regulations.

Market efficiency description of how prices in competitive markets react to new information.

Material an accounting term that means a value is significant to a decision being made.

Merger combination of two or more corporations.

Monetary policy actions by the Federal Reserve Board to control the money supply, bank lending, and interest rates.

NASDAQ National Association of Securities Dealers Automated Quotations. A computerized communications network that provides quotations (bid and asked prices) on stocks.

No-load fund type of mutual fund for which no commission is charged to make a purchase.

OTC market over-the-counter market; trades securities through a centralized computer telephone network that links dealers across the United States.

Poison pill tactic used by corporations to defend against unfriendly takeovers, generally by making a takeover more expensive.

Portfolio an investor's collection of securities owned.

Price/earnings (P/E) ratio ratio of a share's market price to a company's earnings per share.

Prospectus formal written offer to sell securities; includes audited financial statements and other information about the company.

Put option right of a buyer to sell a specified quantity of a security interest at a fixed price at any time during the life of the option.

Registration statement contains a company's financial statements and other information that is filed with the Securities and Exchange Commission each time a new security is offered to the public.

Secondary offering public sale of previously issued securities owned by large investors.

Short sale sale of a borrowed security with the intention of purchasing it later at a lower price.

Spiders index products that track Standard & Poor's 500 Stock Index and are traded on the AMEX.

Statement of cash flows financial statement showing a company's cash receipts and cash payments over a period of time, usually one year.

Stock dividend pro rata distribution of additional shares of stock to stockholders.

Stock market averages average of the market prices of a specified number of stocks; used as a barometer of stock market performance.

Stock split issuance of new shares of stock to stockholders in proportion to the shares they already own.

Stock table summary of the trading activity of individual securities.

Technical analysis process of predicting future stock price movements by analyzing the historical movement of stock prices and supply and demand forces that affect those prices.

Tender offer offer by one company to the stockholders of another company to purchase a specified number of shares at a specified price within a specified time period.

Transer agent an agent, usually a commercial bank, appointed by a corporation to maintain records of stock and bond owners.

Underwriter investment banker who, alone or as a member of an underwriting group or syndicate, agrees to purchase a new issue of securities from an issuer and resell to investors.

Uptick trade transactions executed at a price higher than the previous trade.

Warrant option to buy a specified number of common shares at a predetermined price within a fixed time period.

Webs shares traded on the AMEX that track selected international equity markets.

White knight person or company that saves a corporation from a hostile takeover by taking it over on more favorable terms.

INDEX